SAINT

Saint

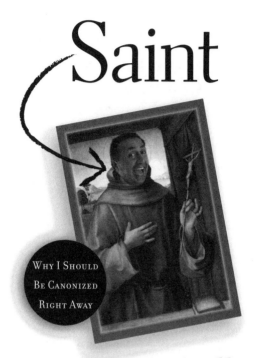

Why I Should
Be Canonized
Right Away

Lino Rulli

SERVANT
BOOKS

PUBLISHED BY FRANCISCAN MEDIA
Cincinnati, Ohio

Unless otherwise noted, Scripture passages have been taken from the *Revised Standard Version*, Catholic edition. Copyright ©1946, 1952, 1971 by the Division of Christian Education of the National Council of the Churches of Christ in the USA. Used by permission. All rights reserved.

Cover and book design by Mark Sullivan.
Photos of the author © Jeffrey Bruno

Library of Congress Cataloging-in-Publication Data
Rulli, Lino.
Saint : why I should be canonized right away / Lino Rulli.
        pages cm
Summary: "Lino's first book,Sinner, was full of stories—honest, humorous, bold, poignant—illustrating why he deserved that title. This new book takes another approach, another angle: why Lino is on his way to sainthood. Often hilarious, but always with a point, Saint focuses on God's grace in Lino's life and shows how even a sinner like him can look forward to being a saint. As Lino himself puts it: "Instead of stories of small triumphs and many failures, this is a book to encourage you in your own triumphs. To realize you might not be as big a sinner as you think. And that with God's help, you might just become a saint." Picking up where Sinner left off, Saint points the way to our end goal: holiness and sainthood. And does so in a way that entertains as well as inspires"— Provided by publisher.
        Includes bibliographical references and index.
        ISBN 978-1-61636-668-1 (pbk.)
    1. Rulli, Lino. 2. Catholics—United States—Biography. I. Title.
        BX4705.R72945A3 2011
        282.092—dc23
        [B]
                                2013024622

ISBN 978-1-61636-668-1

Published by Servant Books, an imprint of
Franciscan Media
28 W. Liberty St.
Cincinnati, OH 45202
www.FranciscanMedia.org

Printed in the United States of America.
Printed on acid-free paper.
13 14 15 16 17   5 4 3 2 1

To My Mom

: CONTENTS :

INTRODUCTION: *Santo Subito, ix*

SERVANT OF GOD

Chapter One: *As for Me and My Lips, We Will Serve the Lord, 3*
Chapter Two: *Bacon: I Like Mine Extra-Crispy, 10*
Chapter Three: *St. Mom, 17*
Chapter Four: *Whatever Happened to…, 26*
Chapter Five: *This Is Going to Hurt. A Lot, 34*
Chapter Six: *Helloooo…, 42*
Chapter Seven: *Benedict the Seventeenth, 49*

VENERABLE

Chapter Eight: *Crybaby, 57*
Chapter Nine: *Sexy Cop, 67*
Chapter Ten: *The Education of a Saint: Five Lessons, 76*
Chapter Eleven: *Are There Any Side Effects?, 88*
Chapter Twelve: *Buona Notte, Nonno, 98*
Chapter Thirteen: *Eating Bad Meat, 106*
Chapter Fourteen: *Dear Diary, 110*

BLESSED

Chapter Fifteen: *Patron of the Arts, 119*
Chapter Sixteen: *St. Lino and His Wacky Companions, 129*
Chapter Seventeen: *My Conscience Is the Only Thing I'm Examining, 136*
Chapter Eighteen: *The Lord Is My Night-Light, 143*
Chapter Nineteen: *Do It Yourself, 153*

Chapter Twenty: *That Is* Not *the Future, 158*

Chapter Twenty-One: *The Soundtrack of My Life, 167*

SAINT

Chapter Twenty-Two: *St. Pat Drives the Ladies out of the Hot Tub, 177*

Chapter Twenty-Three: *Oh Mercy, Mercy Me, 187*

Chapter Twenty-Four: *Aboon Dabashmaya, 197*

Chapter Twenty-Five: *Will You Say Yes?, 205*

Chapter Twenty-Six: *Kiss My Nose, 211*

Chapter Twenty-Seven: *The Reddest Red that Red Had Ever Been, 218*

Chapter Twenty-Eight: *There, 227*

SANTO SUBITO

IT'S APRIL 8, 2005, AND I'm standing on top of one of the colonnades of St. Peter's Basilica. I've got a front-row seat to history: The funeral of Pope John Paul II.

Millions have flocked to St. Peter's. World leaders from every continent (except, strangely, Antarctica). The faithful and not-so-faithful. Maybe even an alien or two floating amongst the mourners—all of them jammed into the piazza. With over a billion people watching from home, this is one of the most viewed television events in history.

I haven't been to many funerals in my life. When I have, none of them turned into pep rallies. Rare is a funeral for someone's Uncle Fred where hundreds of thousands stand, cheering and waving flags. But throughout the funeral for John Paul II, the crowd broke into chants of "Santo Subito!" which means, depending on who's doing the translation, "Sainthood immediately!" or "Sainthood right away!"

Amidst the Catholic-glee, I couldn't help but wonder: Would the crowds at my funeral shout, "Sainthood immediately"? For that matter, would there *be* crowds at my funeral? Would they wave banners in support of my cause? Would my millions of mourners refuse to use the bathroom, lest they lose their spot in the piazza? Would an "I mourned Lino" adult diaper become an instant souvenir?

Would I capture the attention of every major television network on earth? At the very least, would I garner an opening segment on the cable access channel in my hometown of St. Paul, Minnesota?

As of now, very few voices—actually, only the ones in my head—are chanting for my immediate canonization. Yet, I'm left with the fact that Holy Mother Church calls me, somehow, to be a saint. In fact, she calls all of us to holiness, and to be with God in heaven. The discouraging truth for most of us, however, is that the vast majority of canonized saints are priests, nuns or—as in the case of John Paul II—popes. When average Catholics look in the mirror, they don't see a priest, nun, or pope. They don't see a hallowed vision of a future saint. Instead they see a fluorescent-lit reflection of a layperson, a current sinner with all sorts of ugly struggles and failures. When I look in the mirror, I lose my appetite.

So, perhaps inadvertently, the Church is sending a message that only those in the religious life are models of virtue and holiness. That only priests and popes can be canonized. And if that's the case, the consequences are huge: Regular laypeople—that is, the majority of people actually *in* the Catholic Church—don't really believe we're called to be saints.

Some dude who lived in Transylvania in the 1200s and died of the plague might have been holier than holy, but unless he converted Count Dracula, he's not inspiring the majority of us these days.

So I say, canonize *me*. In spite of my shortcomings and horrible mistakes (known in Church circles as "mortal sins"), you could identify with a St. Lino: A guy who does and says lots of stupid things. A saint who took seven spring breaks, though he was in college for only four years. A saint who isn't interested in converting a count—though he does have, oddly, recurring dreams of Count Chocula chasing him with a lawnmower. A saint who celebrates his oddities and failures in the hope that he can encourage his brothers and sisters to join God in heaven. That's me. That's a saint you can relate to.

I titled my last book *Sinner* (available at Amazon.com or wherever fine books are sold). The motivation for that book—other than the handsome advance I was offered—was to share a core message of Christianity: We are all sinners in need of a Savior. Somehow, however, the message backfired. Instead of everyone recognizing his or her own sinful nature, everyone honed in on *my* sinful nature. It turns out that while most folks are uncomfortable with the theological reality that we are all sinners, they're cool with accepting that Lino is a big one.

Case in point: I'm in Rome several times a year. And *Sinner*, to my surprise and pleasure, has been shared throughout the offices and apartments of the Vatican. Yet, to this day, when a certain high-ranking Vatican official, who proudly has a signed copy of my book on his bookshelf, sees me on the street or in the halls of the Vatican itself, he calls out "*Sinner!*" for the whole holy world to hear.

"And with your spirit," I say, in a knee-jerk reaction.

I can't help but wonder if public declarations of my sinfulness—especially those cried out within a stone's throw of the Congregation for the Causes of Saints—aren't hurting my cause for canonization. I hope to undo the damage with this book. In it, I'm making a formal pitch that people stop seeing me as solely a sinner, but also as a saint.

Another motivation for this book is that I'm getting old. I don't like acknowledging that fact, but others seem to have no problem reminding me. I began writing *Saint* ten months ago, on a visit to my alma mater, St. John's University, in Collegeville, Minnesota, which is run by the Benedictines.

During my visit, one of the monks who has known me for twenty years cornered me before evening prayer with an important question: "Where did you get that gray hair?" It was as if he thought it might be contagious and that I should go back to the monastery room to avoid infecting the others. The rest of the evening I wondered the same thing: Where *did* I get this gray hair? I scanned the crowd of monks. Which one had shaken my hand and given me this plague of age?

Weird as it sounds, I still see myself as a twentysomething kid trying to figure out the world. But then I realize how many of my friends are married with kids. Some of their kids are teenagers. A close friend of mine just celebrated his twentieth wedding anniversary. I can't last twenty dates with a woman.

The truth is, there's no one to blame for my gray hair but time. I can no longer be the adolescent waiting for life to figure me out. Instead, I have to be the forty-one-year-old adult who figures life out for himself. And I have to do it soon. It's time to shift the focus from my mistakes and sins to my spiritual growth. I have to answer the Church's call to holiness.

I don't trust my friends to write down an accurate and thorough account of my virtuous life after I die, so I'm doing so now. I hope this book encourages you to focus on your own spiritual growth. To realize that you might not be as big a sinner as you think, and that, with God's help, you might just become a saint.

But let's canonize me first.

: SERVANT OF GOD :

: CHAPTER ONE :

AS FOR ME AND MY LIPS, WE WILL SERVE THE LORD

THE FIRST TIME I KISSED a girl was at the ripe old age of fifteen. The year was 1987, and it all began with a phone call.

"Lino, answer that!" my dad yelled from the living room.

We had two phones in the house. One in my parents' bedroom, which I rarely used lest I accidentally contemplate my conception. The other phone sat on the kitchen counter, keeping the electric can opener company.

Back then, my parents had an odd policy regarding the phone. When it rang, if I was home, I had to answer it. If I wasn't home, one of them would answer it. (Somehow they were unable to muster the strength to pick up the phone themselves when I was there.) And the summer between my sophomore and junior years of high school, I was thrilled whenever the phone rang for me.

"Hello?" I asked, hoping it was for me.

"I'm having a party," my friend Dan said, without even making sure it was I that answered the phone. "It's gonna be a rager," he said confidently.

"My curfew is ten o'clock," I said. "Will the raging be done by then?"

"No. Not late enough," he replied. He seemed annoyed. "Make up a story why you have to stay out later. Lie to your parents."

Lie to my parents just so that I could hang out with Dan and his cassette tapes? I wondered if the lie was worth the hassle.

"It'll be worth it," he said, as if he could read my mind. "My dad bought me a CD player. And girls will be there."

Girls? Not since my mom threw me a tenth birthday bash at Chuck E. Cheese had I been to a full-blown social gathering with girls. I imagined a party like those I'd seen in the movies. *Sixteen Candles. Weird Science. Teen Wolf.* Wild revelry with cars parked like ships scuttled on the front lawn. Inside the house, hundreds of kids jammed into a living room—drinking, smoking, sweating, dancing, and dodging one another's big hair. I might get a chance to destroy a turntable. I might rescue a weeping Molly Ringwald. I might turn into a werewolf. That was the party I wanted to go to.

But I wasn't cool. As it turned out, neither was Dan.

The merrymaking consisted of me, Dan, Phil, three girls I'd never met before, a "gently used" bottle of rum, and a case of Old Milwaukee beer. There was only one car; it was Phil's, parked neatly in the driveway. The six of us began the night sitting around the wood-grained dining room table. The only ones dancing were the collection of porcelain ballerinas crammed in the cabinet behind us. The beast of a boom box, the only macho thing in the room, sat in the middle of the table, unmanned by a doily. Whitesnake pumped from its speakers. We listened, trying hard to pretend that we weren't at the lamest party on the planet. No doubt, even those politically repressed teens we usually pitied way over in the Soviet Union would have been saddened if they could have seen the pathetic condition of this American party.

I was seated between a blonde and a brunette, both as statuesque (I think that's the polite way of saying "big-boned") and strong as I imagined a Soviet girl would be. As I gazed at the brunette to my right, Whitesnake wondered if it was love that I was feeling. Nope. She wasn't the love that I'd been searching for, but she did have a personality, a low tolerance for alcohol, and what seemed like a high tolerance for dorky guys with big noses and even bigger mullets. After her second beer, everything I said was comedy gold. I couldn't go wrong around her. I'd say something mildly amusing, and she'd laugh, which I took as a sign that I should try more jokes.

As a side note, it was moments like this that encouraged me to use my God-given comedic skills only for good. I realized that my ability to throw out a halfway decent joke would be my ticket to success in life. Professionally and personally.

I still recall the first time I ever told a joke in public, and the reaction it got. I was in sixth grade, in my favorite teacher Mrs. McDonald's class. She asked a question about President Lincoln, my classmate Scott answered it, and then she asked if I thought he was right. Pretending to be a drunk in a bar, I lifted up my imaginary glass and said, "I'll drink to that!" It was my first laugh line in public and I can remember the feeling even now. I knew making people laugh was in my future. And now, sitting at Dan's house, I had that feeling again: My ability to crack a joke would pay off…

After one of my unbelievably adequate zingers, she put her hand on my thigh.

"You're so funny, Lino," she said, between guffaws. "Let's go outside."

Did she think my jokes would be even funnier in the driveway? I wondered.

"I want to ask you something out there," she said. Her hand was still on my thigh.

Wow. *Was this girl digging me? Was I finally going to kiss a girl? And, well, with her hand there on my thigh, could I really stand up right now?*

"Sure," I said, knowing I'd need a minute to collect myself. "Be right there."

After I cooled down, my mind struggled to consider the possibilities. Maybe she really liked me. Then again, she said she had a question to ask. I hoped she wouldn't ask about math or geography, because I was horrible at those subjects. Or, even worse, maybe she was going to ask me if Dan or Phil were single. By the time I'd worked through the options, she'd disappeared. I found her outside, standing in front of Phil's car.

"Do you want to kiss me?" she asked with a smile.

"Yessss!" I said so loud and abruptly I scared both of us. I know I scared the dogs in the neighborhood. I might have scared the next-door neighbors, too. Their security lights popped on.

As I approached my Soviet sweetheart, I was going down a road I'd never known. My very first kiss. It was exciting. It was groundbreaking. It was gross.

My lips and tongue were everywhere—her chin, her cheek, her neck— at one point I accidentally licked the top of her hairline. A few times I even hit her mouth. I was a mess.

And while it was clear I had no idea how to kiss a girl, it was also clear I wasn't planning on giving up anytime soon. She was either very patient, found me really attractive, or the Old Milwaukee cancelled all of her judgment capabilities, because she wasn't giving up either. Three hours later, Dan came out to check on us.

"What are you two doing?" He was intrigued. And a little disturbed. "Have you really been making out this whole time?"

We stopped kissing long enough to come up for air and answer him. "Yeah."

Then I shooed him back inside. He could go hang out with his new CD player. I'd waited fifteen years to make out with a girl. I might never have this chance again. I wasn't planning to stop until my lips fell off.

A year would pass before I kissed another girl. It was at another party. This time, we only made out for an hour. Then she made out with my friend Tony. By the time I graduated from high school, I'd kissed a total of two girls. What a stud.

* * *

When I'm canonized, I want to be named the patron saint of kissing.

Ribbon makers have St. Polycarp of Smyrna. Beekeepers have St. Bernard of Clairvaux. Those with bowel disorders have St. Bonaventure. Kissers need someone to intercede for them. Why not me?

You could ask for my prayers the way the absentminded ask St. Anthony's intercessions when they lose something. Only, instead of "Something is lost and can't be found, please, St. Anthony, look around," one could say, "Falling in love would really be bliss, please, St. Lino, get me a kiss!"

If a guy found himself too manly to rhyme, he could try a holier form of prayer: "O loving St. Lino, friend of the single person, please intercede that I may have a first kiss. And that it could lead to a second kiss. And that we may fall in love, if it be the Lord's will."

You want love? God is love. I'll be in heaven with God, and I'll ask Him to give you some. The perfect combination of romance, chivalry, and faith, brought to kissers everywhere by yours truly.

And to sweeten the pot, though I didn't have much experience as a teenager, I've improved my kissing skills a great deal since the 80s (then again, I couldn't get any worse). Now I'm an amazing kisser.

It might sound weirdly confident to acknowledge that I'm a good kisser, but I really am. I don't have that many skills, but that's one of 'em. The women who have kissed me have borne witness—and their testimony is true, and they know that they tell the truth—so that you also may believe.

God gives us gifts He wants us to share. So we Christians need to drop the fake humility when it comes to our talents. If you're a plumber, plumb for Jesus. If you're a dentist, grind away for the Lord. If you're a proctologist, well, glorify Him with your fingers. Jesus made it clear that a lamp is not meant to be hidden under a bushel basket. A lamp is meant to light up the world.

Kissing is my gift. I can light up the world with my lips. I won't pretend that I don't know my way around a set of them. It took time, and plenty of practice, to get where I am today. That's the way it is with most of our God-given talents: Persistence and prayers pay off.

I can see it now, prayer cards featuring a puckered-up St. Lino. Underneath my painted likeness, the motto: "As for me and my lips, we will serve the Lord."

And what happens if my intercessions are so successful that your kissing becomes so good that it can lead to not-so-chaste things? I'm with you on that, too. In me, you have a saint-intercessor who feels your pain.

Wannabe saints, like myself, recognize our own sinful tendencies. And there's no denying that kissing can lead to sin. I've struggled with the sin of lust for most of my life.

Being a lustful person is particularly ironic seeing as I didn't have many opportunities for those sorts of sins when I was younger. Maybe I'm just playing catch-up, since I can't help but feel like I missed out on something during my adolescence. And yet, whatever happened in the past, I have to say no to the pleasures of the flesh all the time. And so do you.

I've come to realize that the ultimate *yes* to God means saying *no* to lots of other things. It's tough saying no. It's not fun saying no. But as Christians, we have to be really good at saying no. Or really good at going to confession.

Matthew 5:37 says, "Let what you say be simply 'Yes' or 'No'; anything more than this comes from the evil one."

I must confess that I spend more time in the confessional than I do at saying no. It's a constant battle raging within me (and within all of us): the pleasures of this life—sex, food, drink, sex, ego, power, sex—versus the pleasures of heaven. Finding moderation and balance in these things takes heroic virtue. And I feel there's a lack of folks up in heaven cheering me on who understand where I'm coming from.

It's my belief that the Church in the twenty-first century needs saints who've made out for three hours in a driveway. That's the real world, and God asks us to live out our holiness in the real world.

So I'll continue to fight the good fight this side of heaven, and when I'm there seated next to the throne of God, I'll happily fight for you, as well.

: CHAPTER TWO :
BACON: I LIKE MINE EXTRA-CRISPY

"ARE YOU JEWISH?" HIS ACCENT was as thick as his beard.

With my swarthy Mediterranean looks, I was tough to profile. To fit in during my trip to Israel, I hadn't shaved in about a month. With my beard, my ethnicity and religion were a crapshoot. I might be Muslim. I might be Christian. I could be Jewish.

"Yes," I said. "That's me. I'm Jewish."

He wasn't convinced. I was wearing a scarf, gloves, and a puffy winter jacket. Wires dangled from my pockets. (Thanks, Steve Jobs, for designing iPod headphones that are as slim as the wires commonly used to fuse suicide bombs.)

It was 2008. The latest intifada was fresh on the minds of the orthodox Jewish rabbis who were conducting interviews near the entrance to the Western Wall, the holiest site in Judaism.

"And where are you from?"

"New York," I said. Unlike the previous lie, this one didn't involve me hiding my Christian faith.

The rabbi transformed from a skeptic into a fan. "New York!" he yelled. "We love our Jewish friends from New York!" Somehow being one of God's chosen wasn't as exciting as hailing from the Big Apple.

"Do you have a *kippah*?" he asked.

Kippah? Hardly know her.

"Um," I stalled. "I forgot mine." Turned out that a *kippah* was the Jewish equivalent of a *zucchetto*, a skullcap, a.k.a. a yarmulke.

My missing kippah put me back in the suspicious category. "But you're Jewish, right?" he asked.

"Yes," I assured him. "Very, very Jewish." Whatever that meant.

"OK," he said, handing me a gently-used-and-hopefully-lice-free cloth circle. I looked around for one of those cans of spray that the guys at the bowling alley use to sanitize the shoes. None to be found. Reluctantly, I put the kippah on my head and followed my rabbi-handler to the section of the Western Wall reserved for the chosen. As I passed by the gentiles, I looked down on them. Get with the Jewish program, folks. Or at the very least, lie.

In the Jewish section, men were reading scrolls. Most of the guys had long beards and wide-brimmed black hats. I think they were reading the Torah, but how should I know? I'm a Christian who hardly reads the Old Testament. There were a few beard-trimmed, temporary-hatted guys like me in the group, but I could tell they were more perusing the words than really praying them.

My rabbi stopped me before I could make it to the wall. "I'm sorry," he said, "I didn't get your name."

Uh-oh. I responded with the first thing that came to my mind: "Lino." *Oy vey*, why did I pick that moment to start telling the truth? I'm used to my name confusing people, but in a religious context, the confusion was unsettling.

"No," he said. "What's your Jewish name?"

I struggled to think of a famous Jewish dude whose name I could borrow. The only one that came to mind was King. As in, King David, King Solomon, Larry King.

I put my hands up in surrender. "You got me," I said. "I'm not Jewish. Not yet. But I'm thinking of becoming Jewish."

He frowned. Apparently, in his book, *thinking* and *becoming* weren't on the same page as *being*.

I offered one more tidbit to help tip the scales in my favor: "I'm already circumcised, if that helps."

It didn't. He wasn't interested in seeing the proof. He pointed in the direction from whence we'd come. "You have to leave—now."

There was nothing left for me to do. "Seems about right," I said, dropping my head and making the walk of shame to the gentile section of the wall.

The massive stones that make up the Western Wall are a remnant of the retaining wall of the ancient Jewish Temple. It was renovated and expanded by Herod the Great. (As in the King Herod who massacred a great number of innocents. Which wasn't so great.) His remodeling work was completely undone, though, by the Romans when they destroyed the Temple in the year 70. As I gazed at the ruins, I thought of my family in Rome. I decided to keep my Roman roots to myself. If anyone asked, I would pretend that my family hailed from France, and that I came from a long line of Rull-*ouis* who had said *yes* for years to running away from the invaders.

Growing up, I know that a priest or religion teacher must have told me about a "Temple," in the city of "Jerusalem," which held the "Ten Commandments." But outside of *Raiders of the Lost Ark*, it never occurred to me that these were real things, let alone things that were first part of a different religion. A religion that regarded the walls of this Temple so holy that the faithful wrote prayers on slips of paper and placed them in the crevices between its ancient blocks.

Out of respect for this tradition, I decided to write the names of all my

Jewish friends and make a prayer on their behalf. I looked at my empty slip of paper. "David," I wrote. Why hadn't I thought to use his name earlier when my rabbi-handler demanded a Jewish name? As one of my closest friends from my days as a broadcaster at the CBS station in Minneapolis, he wouldn't have minded if I'd borrowed his name.

And what other Jewish friends could I add underneath David? Again, my mind went blank. I felt accidentally anti-Semitic.

"Jim," I wrote next. Though Jim doesn't practice Judaism—and, as I recall him telling the story, a well-intentioned nun actually baptized him when he was a baby—nonetheless, he identifies as Jewish, so that counted. Next, I listed some of the famous Jewish folks that I liked. Jerry Seinfeld. Howard Stern. *Was Bruce Springsteen Jewish?* I couldn't remember, but I put his name down, too. Under his, I added Clarence and Little Steven. Pretty sure they weren't Jewish, but were the only E Street Band members I could name.

Done with my list, I jammed my prayers in the nearest crevice, stood back, took a photo, and turned to walk away, trying to remember other Jewish people I knew. And then a name came to me: Max Weinberg! Of course, he's Jewish *and* in the E Street Band! I debated whether or not to return to the wall and add the name.

And then I suddenly remembered another Jewish guy I know: Jesus. He doesn't need my prayers, so no need to go back to the wall and add His name, but I was embarrassed it took so long to remember that Jesus was Jewish.

There have been moments in my Christian life where certain obvious truths of the faith hit me. This was one of those moments. Until then, I had always imagined Jesus as a Catholic, just like me. He got baptized, made His First Communion, fell asleep in CCD, was confirmed, left the Church for a while in His teens and early twenties, and then returned in

His mid-twenties. For you history buffs out there, it turns out that, except for the baptism, I was way wrong.

*   *   *

There's a stone path in the city, near the Church of St. Peter in Gallicantu, so named for the cock that crowed a third time when Peter was done denying Jesus. Archaeologists conclude those stones certainly would have been some that Jesus walked on. His feet touched those steps. As I stood on them, I realized that however a person sees Jesus, this is where He walked.

For Peter: The Jesus who forgave him for his denial—He walked here.

For the believer: The Jesus who lived and died for the salvation of humanity—He walked here.

For the skeptic: The Jesus who was just a super-nice guy, but not God— He walked here.

For the Dan Brown fan: The Jesus who married Mary Magdalene and eventually moved to France—He walked here.

This is the city where He ate and drank, laughed and cried. I can deny Him—and boy, some days I do—but a guy named Jesus was *here*. I can't pretend He never existed, or that He was some mythological centaur. And whoever the man named Jesus was, He was Jewish. His parents were Jewish. His friends were Jewish. And I'm Catholic.

The fact that He was Jewish was summed up, in my immature brain, with one thought: He never ate bacon. And yet here I am, His follower, and I like my bacon extra-crispy. He was like us in all things but sin. And the bacon thing. He wasn't with us on the bacon.

The last day of my trip to Israel, I walked down the Via Dolorosa, the Way of the Cross. It's the path Jesus walked to Calvary on Good Friday. As I followed in His footsteps, I pictured Him carrying the cross on that road. I tried to imagine what was going through His mind in those last hours of His life. This man named Jesus, who didn't eat bacon (*Focus, Lino*), died for our sins.

I ended my journey at the Church of the Holy Sepulchre. It houses some things that are kind of important to Christians, such as the spot where Jesus was crucified and the tomb where He was laid.

The spot where Christ was killed is called Golgotha. I'd heard the word before, but until being there, I never really pictured what it looked like. Or that it was rock. And yet, there it was: The rock of Golgotha. This is the very stone that Jesus' cross stood upon that Friday they call Good. That's insane.

There's a little spot where tourists can go up and feel the actual rock of Golgotha, which put me in a dilemma. Being the germophobe I am, I didn't want to touch it, lest I get some incurable Roman virus that had remained dormant from the first century. Being the Christian I am, I had to at least lay a hand on it.

I walked up and touched Golgotha with my right hand. In my left hand, my trusty bottle of Purell was at the ready.

Virus-free, I then headed over to the tomb of Christ. Out of a reverence for the spot I was entering, I decided to go through on my knees. It was one of my more saintly moments, and since there weren't any tourists around to get in my way, I went forward slowly, one knee at a time. I maneuvered my way into the tomb with the elegance of a six-month-old baby taking his first steps.

It was small in there. Inside, there's a slab where they laid Christ's body. A few candles were burning. There was nothing to say about what happened there almost two thousand years ago, except "It matters."

After a few minutes, other people came along. I immediately got annoyed with them. *Why did they have to ruin my religious moment?*

And then I realized that religious moments are just that. Moments. They don't last forever or they'd be called religious forevers. And so, I soon found myself wondering how long I should stay there for. Plus, I was noticing a tingling in my knees that was a sign that I couldn't handle much more. And then I was wondering if it was necessary for me to go out the way I'd come in, as an infant, or if I could go out walking as an adult. I walked out.

I thought that my visit to Israel would be life-changing. I thought I'd never sin again, because I would be so utterly transformed, but a saint isn't a person who has an experience and is perfect from then on. A saint is someone who takes whatever glimpses of God he or she gets and then builds on those every day.

I was just grateful to have been able to see and share some of the experiences of the Jewish people of the first century. Like them, I can meet Jesus in my sinfulness. But unlike them, I get to eat bacon.

CHAPTER THREE

ST. MOM

IT'S RARE THAT A PARENT
and child are both canonized, but it's happened in the Church's history,
and I'm going to make the argument that it should happen again when
it comes to my mom and I. Or is it mom and me? I'm not sure. I'm not
trying to use proper English, I'm just trying to get properly canonized.

The most famous mother-son saint team is St. Monica and St. Augustine.
Monica, patron saint of mothers (that is, until my mom is canonized and
pushes Monica out), prayed for decades that her son would become a
Catholic. Augustine, of course, went on to become a Catholic and a best-
selling author. (Kinda like me! Except I've always been a Catholic, so I
should get brownie points for that.)

My mother, Gina, is the youngest of three sisters, the only one born in
America. When she was a girl growing up on East Seventh in the Italian
section of St. Paul, Minnesota, her father, Gino, took her to the movies
every Saturday. It's one of the sweetest stories she's ever told me. Why do
I love it? Perhaps it's the image of this tiny version of my mother, holding
her father's hand on the way to the show, Gina e Gino excited to see one
of the cowboy shoot 'em ups that played on the weekends for a quarter
admission. Maybe I like thinking of my mother enjoying the attention an
only child does, an attention I've enjoyed my whole life. In those days, her
older sisters, Maria and Fuvie, were grown up and had already moved out
of the house. Her father could devote all his time to her.

When I'm back in Minnesota, I take Mom to the movies. Of course, she insists on paying. So technically, she's taking me to the movies. But I drive, so that's me taking her. Though we take her car, so it's like she's taking me. But, come to think of it, I bought her that car for Christmas, so, if money is the measure, then I'm taking her. She pays for the popcorn. Once we're in our seats, she pulls out a bottle of water from a purse so large that it could hold a keg. So neither of us pays for that. Clearly, I haven't figured out who's taking whom to the movies. She and I have a complicated relationship, one in which the two of us vie to stay even. She gives; I take. I give; she takes.

Naturally, it wasn't always this way. For most of my life, she gave. I took.

When I was four, Mom was the giver, and in the case of bedtime—the drawer. That's because I wouldn't go to sleep unless she drew me a clown.

"Clown, please?" I'd request, as if she were my own personal Michelangelo.

"It's late, Lino," she'd sigh. "Mom's tired."

This was unacceptable. I was tired too. "How can I go to sleep without a drawing?" I'd ask. I very clearly had said "please." From past experience, she knew I wouldn't be able to fall asleep without gazing on a vision of a man with a grotesquely painted face, a round red nose, and wisps of curly hair peaking out from a derby hat. Never mind the dozens of clown drawings from nights past, all of them dutifully hung on my bedroom walls by the artist, St. Mom.

She pointed to them, pleading, "Can't you just look at one of those, instead?"

Apparently she thought I could be placated by looking at an old clown, one whose value had expired as soon as I closed my eyes the night before. "No," I'd respond. I would fly into a temper tantrum, kicking up the sheets and hollering like Jack Nicholson in *One Flew Over the Cuckoo's*

Nest, writhing until she began work on a fresh masterpiece.

As soon as she started tracing the outlines of the clown face, I mellowed. *More color, please. A little more red on the nose. Fluff up his hair a bit, don't you think? The eyes could be sadder.* When I was satisfied with her work, it went up on the wall with all the other clown portraits, destined to be dismissed in under twenty-four hours.

Eventually, Mom wised up. Not all the way, but at least halfway. She still drew clowns on demand, but she bought a coloring book full of them, allowing her to skip the outline and head right to filling in the colors.

Masterpiece hung, prayers said, Little Lino could go to sleep.

On the road to her canonization, the investigation of my mom's virtues should start, not with the letters she's written, but there in my scrapbook, with the clowns she's drawn.

Perhaps she counted it among God's many mercies that a few years later my obsession with commissioning art gave way to a new nighttime obsession, *The Tonight Show Starring Johnny Carson*. Some weekends my parents would let friends stay overnight for a sleepover, and thus many of my best memories of Johnny include Danny.

Danny, my grade-school buddy who stayed up with me to watch and appreciate the genius of Carson (this was before Letterman, of course, who became the all-time genius). Danny, whom my mom had to drive home the next day. Danny, whose house we could not arrive at until she'd earned one hundred points in a game we devised based on her driving.

The game didn't have a name, but the rules, as with most games that are meant to delay the inevitable, were complicated and ever changing. It went like this: On the way to Danny's house, if she blew by a car on I-94, she earned five points. If, on the other hand, she allowed a car to pass us, she lost five points. "Drive faster!" was our refrain. We kept score in our heads. "Nice! She just passed two cars. That's ten points."

In general, points were rewarded for recklessness and deducted for cautiousness. Rolling through a stop sign earned ten points. Stopping before the white line was a serious deduction. The thrill for me was in trying to persuade her to break the laws of the road. "No one is looking," I'd say. "Gun it." If she wasn't persuaded, I took joy in deducting from her total. "Aww, too bad, you just lost five points there. Looks like we can't drop Danny off yet."

It didn't matter whether Danny's parents were expecting him, whether he had important things to do that weekend—an aunt's funeral to go to, a birthday party to attend—if Mom didn't score one hundred points by the time she reached Danny's house, we had to drive past it until she did.

For the most part, Mom played along with the game. Maybe she enjoyed the recklessness a bit. She was never very adventurous. She never had more than a social drink, and she didn't smoke. Far as I can tell, she has always been happy right where she is. Always patient. Always content. Always at peace. Maybe she liked being rebellious on the road so her son could get his silly hundred points. For being willing to endanger our lives and ruin her driving record, the woman is a saint.

Danny and I lost touch as adults, but I like to imagine him still out there on the freeways of the Twin Cities, recklessly driving in a quest to earn enough points to get home.

* * *

Through junior high, I basically had only two friends: Danny and Keenan. I thought I would be following them to the public high school they were going to—where my mom, coincidentally, taught. Instead, Mom and Pops were insistent that I go to the Catholic high school where I would know no one. And have to wear polyester pants. I protested. I threatened to drop out of high school. I would have channeled Jack Nicholson again, if I'd thought it would work, but Mom was firm.

"You do not want to be at the same high school where your mother works. It wouldn't be fair to you." It occurs to me now that it wouldn't have been fair to her either. She was already responsible for teaching French to a hundred or so teenagers; she didn't need to add managing my escapades to her job description. She stood her ground and turned out to be right, and that took real virtue and perseverance on her part.

Despite my concerns, Catholic high school offered me plenty of opportunities for friendship and hell-raising. On more than one weekend, I came home from a party smelling of alcohol. And tried telling her there was something wrong with her nose. And that what she thought she was smelling she wasn't actually smelling.

"Lino, have you been drinking?" she'd ask as I reached home with just seconds to spare on my curfew.

"Drinking? Me?" I'd ask innocently. "No. It's a new cologne: *eau de Coors*."

And then there was the time she got a call from a police officer friend who informed her that he'd seen me driving recklessly after school. "I didn't pull Lino over because I knew he was your son," he said, "but I won't be able to look the other way again."

"What exactly was he doing?" she asked.

When I got home, she was waiting at the back door for me. "Lino, do you know anything about a guy riding on the roof of your car?"

Of course I knew something about a guy riding on the roof of my car. It was my friend Charlie. If we'd been playing the driving-Danny-home game, the combination of his roof surfing and my driving would have earned us ten thousand points.

"Nope," I said. "I don't know anything about it."

"You sure there wasn't a young man standing on top of your car yesterday?"

She was blocking my way to the kitchen, so I tried what I always try when I'm caught in a lie—I went on the offense. "You think I wouldn't know if someone was on the roof of my car?"

Mom didn't back down. "Make sure it doesn't happen again."

I got the message. No more friends on the top of my car. She grew in holiness. Although…she didn't say anything about *me* on the top of the car.

*   *   *

In college, I gained so much weight I wouldn't have been able to hoist myself onto the top of my Nissan Sentra without putting a serious dent in the roof. I was the same 5'8" I'd been when I graduated high school, but I'd gone from 130 to over 200 pounds. Maybe it had something to do with what I was eating. My standard McDonald's order consisted of two double cheeseburgers and a large order of fries. When I wanted to eat healthy, I'd go to Subway and get a footlong Spicy Italian and a six-inch meatball sub. And who knew beer had calories?

Christmas break during my senior year, Mom casually mentioned that I'd put on a few pounds. She was concerned about me, as always—this time about my eating and drinking.

"Don't worry," I reassured her. "It's just college."

She couldn't change me. She couldn't control what I ate or drank. I was now an adult, free to make my own bad decisions. So instead, she did the next best thing: Tell me she was concerned, but love me, nonetheless.

After college and grad school, I moved back home so that she could get a front-row seat for the matinee showing of *Lino Doesn't Want to Work.*

"You have to get a job," she said, when, after being out of work for three months, she saw no signs that I was intending to do so.

"You don't understand," I said. "I'm different from everyone else." I tried to put my uniqueness in simple terms: "I can only work at a job that I love."

"It's not a question of if you love the job or not," she said. That's what people do: They work."

Work was what Mom had done when she graduated from college. It's what Pops had done when he graduated from college.

But their offspring was different.

"At least get a temp job."

Mom handed me a slip of paper on which she'd written the number of a place called Manpower.

"Is this a gay bar?" I asked.

My dad stepped on my laugh line. "If I tell you to work at a job you hate for the rest of your life you're going to do that and say 'thank you' and ask for overtime."

"Why would I ask for overtime at a job I hate?" I said.

He continued. "You're going to get a job tomorrow, or else..."

He didn't have an "or else" because, as usual, he was yelling with a mouthful of pasta.

Manpower turned out to be a temporary employment agency, and I got a job at a soap company doing sales analysis for a few months. A salesman would say he sold thirty packs of soap, I'd check the invoice to verify it, and he'd get his commission. I'd then take a smoke break—even though I didn't smoke—and an even longer lunch break with my buddy Pat, who'd also been lucky enough to land a temp job there. We'd get lunch, stop at an arcade and play air hockey, get busted by our bosses for slacking off, and head back to work.

Every night, I'd come home and remind my parents that my days at the soap company were numbered. I wasn't going to do a job like everyone else for the rest of my life.

To my parents' surprise—but certainly not my surprise—I proved myself right and found a career that I love: Working in the media. First, it was hosting my own TV show. Then, it was as a television reporter. And less than fifteen years after playing air hockey with my buddy Pat on lunch breaks from my job at the soap company, I took a job in New York broadcasting for SiriusXM Satellite Radio's *The Catholic Channel*, where I happily take long lunch breaks with cohost, Fr. Rob Keighron, and my buddies from *The Howard Stern Show*. We haven't found any arcades in New York that have air hockey, though. Yet.

When I told my mom about the New York opportunity, she was happy for me, of course, but sad for her.

"I won't have you around," she said. "I can't be a mom without my son."

It's one of her classic one-two punches, the kind of line that knocks the wind out of me and simultaneously builds me up.

My parents wanted me to work—whether I loved or hated a job—and it turns out, I love working. In fact, I care too much about my work. I'm never completely satisfied with what I do; it's never quite enough with me. *I'm* never quite enough. And so, the bittersweet part of the story is that I proved myself right. To my own peril. I know Mom doesn't like seeing how much I work. I'm sure that's painful for a parent to deal with.

I call her every night, and when she senses my anxiety, she says she wishes there was something she could do to help. There isn't, and she gets that. But she offers anyway. That's a saint.

So my constant prayer for her is: "Lord, let my mom live long enough to see her son happy and at peace."

But perhaps her greatest and most saintly quality of all is that she has never once nagged me about settling down and getting married.

I know how happy she'd be to see me in love. To see me standing at the front of the little wedding chapel in St. Peter's Basilica where I've always said I'll get married. And I know she'd be a loving grandmother. I'd give her grandchildren she could draw a new generation of clowns for, and she'd look, with love in her eyes, at me struggling to be a parent. In truth,

I can't help but feel I've completely let her down in this regard. Things between us are uneven.

* * *

My mom isn't my best friend. She and I both agree that it would be weird if she were. Still, I try to spend time with her when I can. I've offered to take her to some of the more exotic places on earth that I've been to, but she really doesn't want to go.

"I live vicariously through you," she says. I think she just doesn't want to get all the vaccinations.

And so, someplace along the way in my travels, I'll visit a church or religious site and buy her a little piece of art to hang on her wall. She now has dozens of these mementos from places I've been. Perhaps it's my way of paying the debt I owe her for all the clowns she's drawn.

But Italy is where we travel together. We go there once or twice a year, and in the midst of the shopping and eating, we visit churches.

Each time we enter one of Rome's great basilicas, she'll ask, "Have we ever been here before?" We have. Probably fifty times.

If she were someone else's mom, I'd think her mind was slipping. But this is who she is and has always been. Prayers, not churches, are what she chooses to remember. And it's pretty cool for her, because each time we go, it's like visiting them for the first time.

There I'll be, in the middle of pointing out the same few things I always point out in whatever church we're in, and I'll look around and find my mom, tiny St. Mom, kneeling in a pew, her eyes closed, praying.

It's the best proof of God that I have: Mom in prayer. I love my mom so much that, quite frankly, I wish I had the kind of love for God that I have for her. Maybe someday.

But till that day, I can't help but think that my reckless drive for heaven is an attempt to earn enough points so that I can spend an eternity not just with God, but with her. She'll be my favorite saint in heaven.

CHAPTER FOUR

WHATEVER HAPPENED TO...

MY CAREER IN BROADCASTING HAS taken many twists and turns. There have been hills and valleys. And if I hadn't become a Catholic media superstar, what would I be doing? That's easy. I'd be a rapper.

By my freshman year of college, I'd become a huge fan of rap. NWA, Run–D.M.C., Beastie Boys, Tone Loc…OK, Tone Loc was a bad choice and I'm sorry about that. But I loved rap. There were days I so wished I was black. Granted, the Beastie Boys were white, but I kinda thought they wanted to be black, too.

I'd throw hints at my wannabe status all the time. An LA Raiders hat, like the guys from NWA would wear. Adidas on my feet like Run-D.M.C. You could even see me walking around campus wearing a Howard University T-shirt (it was, after all, a predominantly African American university) that simply said "Howard." My white friends could mock me all they wanted: *Hey Lino! Howard called and he wants his shirt back!*

But one guy who didn't make fun of my clothes was my friend Derek. He got my choice in fashion—and my choice in music. Thankfully, he was black. And we formed a rap duo.

To get a show on our college radio station, we first had to come up with rap names. His came easily: D-Love. That's cool, right? He was just naturally a smooth character. I, on the other hand, was too lazy to decide on a dope rap name that would attract the fly honeys. And so I became "Lazy Lin."

And thus began my career in broadcasting. On a college radio station with less wattage than a microwave, *D-Love and Lazy Lin's Show of Pleasure* aired weekly. Some would say very weakly. An hour of rap and hip-hop, with our commentary shoehorned in.

"Yo, all the way from Brooklyn, these are your boys, Third Bass! And they are dope! This song is off the hook, yo, it's 'Pop Goes the Weasel,' so check 'em out, y'all..."

D-Love and I eventually evolved from our roles as DJs to become artists. We knew a guy with a home studio who agreed to let us use his microphones and recording equipment, and in return all we had to do was pay him. Sounded like a good deal to us newbies in the business. Together, we wrote and recorded a song called "Whatever Happened To," a retrospective that looked all the way back to the mid-80s. Keep in mind this was 1991, so we wouldn't be looking all that far back. Feel free to rap along if you know how it goes:

LL: Whatever happened to phrases like "cool and "fresh"?

DL: Whatever happened to girls showin' all the flesh?

LL: I don't know, but things sure have changed, rearranged, and played tricks on my brain.

LL & DL: So here we are kickin' it freestyle. Two brothers makin' the ladies go...wild.

DL: Wild is what we are. We don't play guitar.

LL: But we do like to chill with the girls at the bar.

DL: Diff'rent Strokes, What's Happenin', What's Happenin' Now.

LL: Man that crazy sucker Rerun really could chow...

DL: Bowl after bowl of Lucky Charms cereal.

LL: What?

DL: It doesn't matter, man; it's immaterial. The past is the past, but the future is ours.

LL: Yo, knock that off, let's go to the bar.

DL: Step, this is a message that must be heard. Through comical lyrics that may sound absurd.

LL: But inside there's a message and the message is word, so open up your ears or get kicked to the curb.

DL: And so, it's just a matter of fact,

LL: It's not where you're from, it's where you're at…

You probably didn't hear it on your local radio station. That's because the only radio station to play it was our local college radio station. On our show. Even we didn't play the song in very heavy rotation, however. And since it never made it on *Yo MTV Raps!*, the world premiere of the song just happened—in this book.

In addition to the rhythm and the rhyme, I was attracted to rap because it stood against power. My fight against The Man was something I struggled with throughout my teens and early twenties. For a long time, I thought The Man was holding me down. Trying to stifle me. And as a Catholic, The Man was the Church. Or, since we refer to the Church as feminine, it was The Woman holding me down. Which sounds kinky. But still restrictive.

There were so many subjects I took issue with when it came to Church: women priests, going to Mass every week, papal infallibility. The list was so long, I could have composed a rap song of my grievances. But it's tough to make anything rhyme with the word *infallibility*.

I was torn. As a rapper, my nature was to rebel. But as a Catholic, I believed there was a Supreme Power in heaven and on earth. So ultimately, I surrendered. Both to the will of God and to the notion that I was a rapper.

* * *

I didn't stop thinking there was a chance I was black until I moved to Nassau, Bahamas, to teach at a Catholic high school. The island's population was more than 90 percent black. (And by the way, for the politically correct among us who might be wondering why I don't say African American: This wasn't America. This was the Bahamas. They were Bahamians, not Americans. And no one says African Bahamian.)

I lived near a monastery, and I stopped by regularly for meals. My roommate at the time, a white guy named Rich, was usually with me. One day he stopped by the monastery without me. The housekeeper noticed that I wasn't with him.

"Where's your friend?" she asked.

"Who, Lino?" he responded, as if he had other friends.

"Yeah, the Chinese one," she clarified.

"Chinese? Lino? The guy with the big nose?"

"Yeah, that's the one. He ain't Chinese?" she asked, surprised.

I was a white guy who kinda thought he was black who got mistaken for being Chinese. It was a confusing time. It seemed that no one on the island knew what I was, not even the tourists.

I bumped into a famous tourist while walking along the beach on the north side of Paradise Island: Sean Combs, as in "Puffy." Or P. Diddy. Or just Diddy. Or Sean John. I've always had a tough time knowing what he wants to be called.

"Hey, you know where I can rent Jet Skis?" he asked, presuming I was a fellow vacationer.

I tried to play it cool. "I can hook you up with my man Everett. He'll give you a good deal."

"Oh, you know someone?" I wondered why he'd asked for help if he didn't expect it. "Great. How long you here on vacation?"

"No, I live here. So I've got this view all the time." The sin of pride has always been with me.

"You live here? But you're…"

I finished the sentence for him. "…white. I know."

He looked at me more carefully. Probably admiring my tan. "You are white, right?"

So I learned what it meant to be white. Black. And Chinese. But more important than what I learned about race, I learned what it meant to be Christian.

Being raised Roman Catholic, if you'd have asked me if I was a Christian, I would have answered, "Nope, I'm Catholic." I didn't get that Catholics were the first Christians. Or, that the word *catholic* means "universal." It never occurred to me that Catholics were Christians too. I saw Christians as "others." We're Catholics. They're Christians.

Spending time among the Christians I met in the Bahamas, I learned what it meant to be Christian, not just in name, but in actions. Before that, I'd been a Catholic like I'd been a rapper. I wore the outfits and the jewelry, I knew the lyrics to the songs, but I didn't really live it.

I didn't know much about the Bible, whereas the kids I was teaching could quote Revelation. I was afraid to pray in public, and they couldn't get enough of it. At their core, they lived the faith. I sat back and experienced it on Sundays.

These high-school kids inspired me to pray, to be bold in my faith, and even to take on things I never thought I could do. Like become a coach. The varsity boys' soccer team needed one. Being Italian, I felt like soccer was in my blood. But being Italian American, I didn't really know any of the rules. So I did what any pseudo-expert does: I studied.

I bought a Pele videotape, and memorized every move and play. I bought the most expensive soccer shoes I could find. And I hit the field.

Our first day I got the guys together for a scrimmage, just to get them to kick the ball around so I could assess their talent.

"You gonna join us, Coach?" one of the players asked. I was determined that I didn't want to be the hypocritical preacher who says one thing but lives another way, so I thought it best to go out and show I play soccer like I coach. Thanks to my studies, and the fact that the guys didn't want to make the new coach look bad, I scored a goal within the first two minutes. *That should show these kids who's boss,* I thought. And they seemed pleased to have a coach who knew his way around the field. I heard one of the midfielders say, "Rulli knows how to play, eh?"

I was proud of myself.

A few plays later, I made a move on one of the defensemen. Todd was a track-and-field star, new to playing soccer, so it was easy to deke him out (a phrase I learned from my soccer studies). I gave a head bob to the right, pushed the ball through his legs and easily got past him. As I moved the ball upfield, I forgot that Todd was fast...really fast. He raced up to me within seconds and took a good kick at the ball. Unfortunately for me, he missed and made contact with my right ankle instead. The pop was quite audible.

As I lay on the ground, writhing in pain, I overheard more than one disparaging comment about the new coach. "Rulli cries like a girl, eh?"

I'd suffered a hairline fracture on our first day of scrimmaging. Thus, I decided from then on that it might be best if I stayed on the sidelines and coached. First rule: Todd was to stay with the opposing team's best players when we needed to get rid of them. I was living proof that he didn't know the difference between an ankle and a ball, so a ref shouldn't give him a red card and eject him.

Before our first game, I quietly asked if we should pray, and I found out they were as competitive in their prayers as they were on the field.

In time, I had to make a flow chart to determine who would get to pray before each game.

"Father God," our goalie, Casey, began. He had the fervor of a televangelist. "We want to thank you, Father God, for the gifts and abilities You have given us. Bless us, Father God, with health and safety—for us and for our opponent—that all we do may glorify Your name. In Jesus' name, we pray. Amen."

Whoa. That's a prayer. He meant it, too. It wasn't some repetitive Catholic prayer that I would have said when I was his age.

I could tell from the sincere faith of these players that defining success with this team wouldn't be about winning or losing. It would be about prayer. Fellowship. And, well, who am I kidding…winning. I won't take you through the *Hoosiers* story line. It's enough to say that we won the national championship. And though the nation was not as large as most, the school had been around for fifty years without winning a trophy. Until Coach Rulli and his delicate ankle showed up. Perhaps my favorite part of the victory came after the game, in the *Nassau Guardian—the* newspaper of the Bahamas:

> Guardian Sports Reporter:
> May 13, 1996
> Forward Lavarde Rolle scored Saint Augustine's College's lone goal in sudden-death overtime on Saturday to lift the Big Red Machine over the Queens College Comets to victory…
>
> He also thanked their coach, Mr. Rulli, who he said stuck by the team through thick and thin.
>
> "He just came to SAC this year and he stuck by us all the way. He helped us along, and we want to thank him, as he has always told us to play team soccer—and on Saturday what we basically tried to do was to do as he said, and control the ball in defense,

bring it to the midfield and work it up that way. He was there for us," added Damani Horton.

When I was coaching that team, I looked at every day as a new opportunity to grow in virtue. Not just by keeping some sort of a checklist: "Did I lust today?" or, "Did I show forgiveness today?" But instead by seeing every hour as an opportunity to be more like Christ. I wanted to be there for my students. I wanted to be there for God.

By the end of my teaching year, when it was time for me to leave the Bahamas and try out a new adventure, I had become a Catholic Evangelical. Most Catholics aren't good at that born-again stuff, but I was picking it up quickly. I was thanking God for what He'd given me. I was compassionate with my players when they weren't at their best. We said grace before every meal. We prayed, and laughed, and worshiped as if we were part of the early Church.

Some of my former students are now pastors, with their own churches. I remember one of them, in particular, asking me, "How long you been a Christian for?"

"Well, I guess all my life." I said, a bit confused by the question. "You?"

"Me? I've been a Christian seven years, four months, twenty-five days, and about three hours."

I've never been black. Sometimes I don't look white. But, as of this writing, I've been a Christian struggling to be who God called me to be—a saint—for forty-one years, 191 days, and six hours. And being a saint—like being a rapper—means being countercultural while still knowing your own cultural heritage. As Lazy Lin would say back in the day: Word.

CHAPTER FIVE

THIS IS GOING TO HURT. A LOT.

WHEN I WAS FIVE, THE Rulli clan decided to try something we had never tried before (or since): a family reunion. Why we needed to make a midsummer exodus from where we all lived to a farm in Wisconsin is a mystery. To this day, no one can remember why we chose the farm. Or who even owned the farm.

The idea of big-city Italians on a farm brings to mind a strange vision of Frankie the Farmer selling his wares at the local vegetable stand: "Hey, this corn just fell off the back of a truck. Who wants some?" Perhaps the farm was owned by a guy we mistook for a member of the family on account of his greasy skin and neck full of gold jewelry that embellished the bib of his overalls.

As happens in most family reunions, by the first day the Rullis had aligned themselves into two factions—the insiders and the outsiders. The insiders watched TV and enjoyed the air conditioning, while the outsiders barbecued and did whatever else one does in the messy outdoors. I quickly aligned myself with the adults inside, sitting on a couch that was so musty it might as well have been a hay bale, eating string cheese and watching *Hee Haw*. Why was I watching *Hee Haw*, a show based on a farm, while I could have left the couch and actually been on a farm? Another of life's mysteries.

"Come on, Lino," my cousin Mike said. He'd joined the outsiders early, riding a motorbike around the farm's open fields. "Let's go for a ride."

Mike was Uncle Joe's son, eight years older than me and always doing adventurous stuff.

"I don't know," I said, concerned about switching my allegiance.

He blocked my view of the TV. "It'll be a blast," he promised. "You'll be back here before you know it." I've always been a sucker for peer pressure. As soon as the show went to commercial, I agreed to Mike's plan.

Did any of the adults notice Little Lino leaving? My parents were there. Mike's parents were there. So were the other insiders, relatives so distant that I didn't know who they all were. Did any of them wonder where I was going and if I'd be safe?

Outside, Mike rolled the bike into the yard, hopped on the front and told me to jump on the back. Although I was already a bit of a control freak, I didn't know how to drive a motorcycle so I put my life in Mike's hands.

On the plus side, the bike looked safe. And it was. Very, very safe. Unless you happened to be sitting behind the driver and the driver revved the throttle, and the engine came alive, and the driver put it in gear, and the bike was chain-driven, and you happened to dangle your left leg in the only place it could dangle—against the uncovered chain.

I recognized the problem when, about three seconds into the ride, the chain chewed up my calf all the way to the bone.

Mike recognized the problem too, turning off the engine and helping me off the bike. The two of us looked at my leg, nearly cut in half lengthwise. I didn't say a word. Accidents didn't happen on *Hee Haw*. I was missing my TV and cheese. And, by the looks of it, I was now missing part of my leg.

"Wow," one of my cousins, an outsider, yelled. "That must hurt!"

"Lino, does it hurt?" another one asked.

In an emergency, the Rullis are an intelligent and sensitive bunch.

My parents appeared, looking at the damage to my leg. My dad asked, "Should we go to the hospital?"

Even to five-year-old me, this seemed like a reasonable option, considering, you know, that my leg was split open like a hoagie roll.

Mike was excited about the prospect of taking me. "He can hop back on the bike, and we'll be there in no time."

I shook my head. After a three-second joyride on the motorcycle, I wasn't up for another ride. "Too soon," I told him. Plus, I didn't trust that Mike even knew where a hospital was.

Then there was a debate about who would have to stop enjoying this beautiful summer day to take me all the way to the hospital. Their indecision hurt almost as much as the gash on my leg did.

My family cast lots as if they were the first disciples of Christ, looking to see which one of them would take the place of Mike, the loser martyring him- or herself with a trip to the hospital. My Uncle Joe was chosen, which seemed only fair since it was his son who had gotten me into this mess. I sat in the front seat of his car, my leg propped up on his dashboard, bouncing as we sped down dirt roads that led from the farm to Vince Lombardi General Hospital, or Our Lady of the Holy Cheesehead. I can't remember the name.

I do remember the doctor who put me on a gurney and took out a needle that was about the size of...*me*. Up to that point in my short life, my experience with doctors was that they tried to paint a rosy picture of the hell that was about to come.

Doctors were different in Wisconsin. "I have to inject this directly into the wound," he said to my Uncle Joe, as if asking his permission. And to me, "This is going to hurt. A lot."

I blacked out. That was 1977.

Yet I'm reminded of that fine afternoon every time I look at my left leg and the giant scar that's still there. Something I would learn later in life, with each successive injury, is that I don't heal well.

* * *

Sometimes I think my Uncle Joe had a hand in my injury. That perhaps, like the head of the Rulli Cosa Nostra, he'd decided the family couldn't tolerate a *Hee-Haw*-loving cousin messing up "our thing." He had tried to use my cousin, his oldest son, to snuff me out. When Mike failed in his mission, Uncle Joe was disappointed but not deterred. When I was sixteen, he tried again. This time, he got a professional to do the dirty work: me.

At first, I enjoyed the produce department job that he got me. It was a colorful place to work, not because of the fruits and vegetables, but because of my coworker Gary. He was in his early twenties, and though he was in great physical shape, he was prematurely balding. He reacted to his follicly-challenged circumstances the way most guys in his situation do—he tried to jam in all the fun with the ladies before it was too late.

Each shift, as I unpacked crates of lettuce and cucumbers, Gary shared his stories of sexual conquest. In. Graphic. Detail. Using the various props readily available in the produce section to help him illustrate the action.

He always began his stories in *Penthouse Forum* letter fashion: "I never thought I'd be telling a story like this," he'd say. I wasn't fooled by the fake hesitation. All he *did* was tell stories like this.

One day a shipment of bananas came in, and I was given the tedious task of opening all the boxes with my trusty box cutter. While I worked, Gary got busy in the vegetable section, using a set of watermelons to demonstrate a particular story. I had just placed a box of bananas on a cart, and—as I always did—I placed my left hand on top of the box, held the box steady, and with my right hand cut off the top section of the box. Unfortunately, instead of cutting the box open, I accidentally slid the blade down the length of my left thumb.

"Oh no!" I said.

Gary dropped the watermelons on the ground—they burst open in a way that would have made Gallagher proud—and rushed over to me. "What happened?" he asked.

I showed him the open wound on my once-opposable thumb. "I just about cut my thumb off!"

They say that the measure of a man is how he responds to crisis. With the quick thinking of a battlefield medic, Gary raised my hand, assessed the gash, and grabbed a towel to wrap around my thumb. Though he was a goof, Gary was a real man under pressure. I, unfortunately, was not.

I went into shock. "Is this really happening to me?" I cried.

"Yeah," he said, chuckling. "Sorry, I don't mean to laugh."

"This can't be happening to me. I have my whole life ahead of me."

"Relax, bud. It happens to the best of us. Maybe you'll have a hot nurse at the hospital who will…"

"Not now, Gary," I shushed him with my four-fingered hand. "What a nightmare. What a disaster. What a nightmare-disaster." I was hyperventilating, hyper-hyphenating my words, and Gary was pestering me with the not-so-distant possibility that I would be in the finer-than-fine presence of a sexy nurse.

He called someone to get the manager, attempting to distract me with stories while we waited. "I hooked up with a sexy nurse once, and let me tell you, she gave me the cure for what was ailing me, if you know what I mean."

When the general manager, a good friend of my Uncle Joe's, showed up, the two of them rushed me to the parking lot and into his yellow Chevy Camaro IROC-Z.

Gary was excited about the ride. "This baby handles like a dream."

Normally I'd be psyched, too, but all I could think of was the far-reaching consequences of my injury.

"I'll never be able to drive again," I said. "My life is ruined. I'll never be a hand model."

This got their attention. "You want to be a hand model?" Gary asked.

I moved on to the sports I'd never pursue. "I'll never swim again."

"Speaking of swimming," Gary said, "I hooked up with this smoking hot lifeguard the other night. I told her, 'Baby, you can give me mouth-to-mouth anytime.'"

I wasn't going to let him interrupt my drama. "What if they can't stitch it up and they have to amputate my thumb? My hitchhiking days are over!" My mind was all over the place. Gary's mind, however, was still on one thing.

"Did I ever tell you about the time I picked up these two cute hitch-hikers on the side of the road? They didn't have gas money, but they paid me in other ways, if you know what I mean."

It was the general manager who got Gary to temporarily knock it off. "Of course we know what you mean. We always know what you mean."

At the hospital, I was informed by a not-so-sexy doctor that I needed twenty stitches to suture the wound, one for every story Gary told me while I was being stitched up.

*   *   *

Though I didn't lose my leg or my thumb, I'm still left with the scars. Strangely enough, it's rare that anyone points them out. I don't hide them, and I don't think people are uncomfortable bringing them up. Instead, I think it's that no one notices them the way I do. After dating her for a year, with plenty of hand holding, my girlfriend at the time once asked, "Hey, when did you cut your thumb?" Another friend that I'd known for ten years asked on a boat trip, "Hey, what's that huge scar on your leg from?" For both of them, my scars were a revelation.

Part of this is because I heal poorly. If I get a paper cut today, the wound will be with me for months. I've got bad skin, I guess. And, over time, I've realized this is a metaphor for my life: Like my physical scars, the emotional scars in my life aren't evident to anyone else. I'm constantly aware of them though, and it turns out I have an even harder time healing emotionally than I do physically. It seems the older I get, the more conscious I am of my scars.

When I was in my twenties, I went to a bar with my friend Jeff. We spotted two cute girls we wanted to meet. I walked up to the brunette. "Hi," I said. "Where are you from?" It wasn't even close to a Gary-inspired pickup line. She looked at me and said one word: "Loser."

Either she was from a town called Loser, or she called me one. Maybe she was having a bad day, maybe she had her own scars, but I can still feel the pain as if it's happening all over again.

I've worked in television and radio since 1998, and I can remember almost every piece of hate mail I've received. Letters and e-mails that describe me as a "disgrace," an "embarrassment," a "heretic"—and those are just from family members.

Last year I got an e-mail to top all e-mails: A guy who'd listened to the radio show for a while wrote to tell me he wished I would have a heart attack. To be fair to him, he gave me options: "I hope you have a mild stroke or a heart attack," he said.

I make jokes about such things, but these are the scars that I carry with me every day. You *might* see my physical scars. My sarcasm and occasionally cruel jokes are probably a reaction to my own emotional scars. But then there are the spiritual scars.

In prayer, I ask God lots of questions. "Where are you?" "Why don't you protect me more?" "If you love me so much, why do I feel so hurt some days?" Sometimes I feel God has just completely let me down when

He doesn't answer my prayers the way I want Him to. He's let friends and family members die. He's kept me from achieving all of my career goals. So many times I've turned to God and said, "Help me!"—only to get silence in return. And that silence can open up new scars—scars that are roadblocks in prayer. It's what makes faith so difficult for me: all the unhealed spiritual and emotional injuries throughout my life.

I'd come up with this idea of spiritual scars a few years ago while standing in line for the sacrament of reconciliation. I was preparing to confess the sins of lust, pride, ego, and jealousy for the thousandth time—which, by the way, would make for a neat celebration...maybe a parade with confetti and a key to the confessional, uh, I mean city—and I suddenly realized that while I needed God's forgiveness...I also needed to forgive myself.

When I confess contritely, with a firm resolve to go and sin no more, my sins are as far from me as the east is from the west. (Ask anyone in a gang, and they'll tell you: East Coast and West Coast are worlds apart.)

Still, some of my open wounds stem from my inability to forgive myself. Turns out, God forgives more easily than I do.

*I never thought I'd be writing a story that ends like this...*one in which I admit that even though God forgives me of my sins, the scars still remain. However, a saint is the person who, in spite of the hurt, in spite of the scars, risks it by being open to being hurt again. By God, by loved ones, by girls at bars, and by family members without motorcycle permits.

: CHAPTER SIX :

HELLOOOO...

ONE OF THE SINS I struggle with is jealousy.

Well, saying I struggle with jealousy is like saying a fat guy struggles with eating pizza. The problem isn't the struggle. The problem is that the pizza always wins. And in my life, jealousy always wins. For the past ten years, I can't think of the last time I went to the sacrament of reconciliation *without* confessing the sin of jealousy. In fact, I'm actually jealous of anyone who can go to confession without confessing that sin. (Which means I just committed the sin of jealousy again. And damn, I just went to confession two hours ago. Not joking.)

Hosting my radio show allows me to meet people I'm jealous of all the time. And I've found that there's two kinds of jealousy: healthy and unhealthy. Here's a short list of folks I'm healthily (that is, not sinfully) jealous of:

Mark Wahlberg is, by far, the coolest guy I've ever met. He's an A-list star, of course. He's been in great films, he's in incredible shape, and I don't know anything about the guy that doesn't cause jealousy. What makes me most jealous about the guy is that he wakes up every morning and prays. He told me he goes to church every day—if not daily Mass, he at least makes it into the doors of a church, regardless of where he is in the world. He wears a rosary. I think, ultimately, I'm jealous that he's got his priorities in place. He's totally committed to God, and I wish I were as committed.

Then there's Derek Jeter. Who's got it better than that guy? I hate playing baseball, and he makes me want to be a baseball player. Every question I asked him on the air made me sound stupid and him sound cool. He's just cool. His handshake is cool, his way of taking a picture with me was cool, and his cool was cool. I'm jealous of cool.

When I met Kim Kardashian, I was jealous that everyone wanted to look at her butt. I have no butt. (Well, I have a butt, but no one wants to look at it.) I'm more interested in a woman's face than I am the sum of a woman's parts...but that was sum butt. She was surprisingly nice—though I wasn't sure what her talents or reasons for fame were, which caused me more jealousy. She's a million times more well known than me. But I don't know why.

When I had Ed McMahon on my show, God rest his soul, I was jealous because he got to sit next to Johnny Carson for all those decades. A front-row seat to comedy history in the making—and he got paid to laugh! Nowadays, there are a dozen late-night talk show hosts. Back then, there was only one: Johnny. I'm jealous that he got to live in a time and a place of appointment television. Before DVR, before cable, and, for that matter, before color television, he was there. I love the television medium so much, and to be seated next to a legend for that many years? If I wasn't jealous of him, I wouldn't be human.

We had Martin Sheen and Emilio Estevez on the show, and we hung out for about fifteen minutes just chatting before going on the air with them. I wasn't actually jealous of them. They were great guys. Instead, I was jealous of my cohost Fr. Rob, because Martin definitely liked Fr. Rob more than he liked me. I mean, Martin was really nice to me and laughed at all my jokes. But he and Fr. Rob bonded like they were old friends. (Nonetheless, Martin autographed a book for only one of us. That'd be me. So Fr. Rob is at least jealous about that.)

I could go on and on—and in my head, there's a constant loop running of who I'm jealous of and why—but it's healthy for me to meet folks I'd otherwise be jealous of because it makes other people jealous of me. Which makes me feel better about myself.

This obsession I have with jealousy extends well past celebrities, unfortunately. Happily married people? I'm jealous they're in such a healthy relationship. Unhappily married people? I'm jealous they have a chance to turn things around.

I'm jealous of people who are less popular than me, since they somehow are at peace with being less famous than me. And I'm jealous of people more popular than me, because they get to be at peace with being more famous than me.

And I have a weird, non-sinful jealousy thing going on with saints. There are saints who lived holy lives: I'm jealous of them if their faith and holiness came easily. As much as I sarcastically comment on the men and women who were tucked away in monasteries and convents, far from the real world and its struggles, I'm jealous that they had that vocation to begin with. Most of us are way too antsy to lock ourselves into a cloister for the rest of our lives. So, while I'm jealous of those saints, there's yet another group of saints I envy even more. That's because they really didn't do much of anything until…

Jesus showed up.

I'm not talking about the men and women who saw Jesus for the few weeks after His resurrection. I'm talking about the folks who were going about their lives and suddenly…*boom!* It's Jesus.

St. Faustina Kowalska comes to mind. If you don't know much about her, join the club. But I'll tell you what I know of her story, nonetheless.

As you can tell by the name, she was Asian. Oh, I'm sorry, I got that wrong. Polish.

I went to Poland a few years ago, as kind of a "footsteps of John Paul II" trip. I started in Wadowice, his little hometown. I visited the house where he was born, which is now a museum filled with random artifacts like his bathrobe and slippers—complete with papal crest! Across the street, I stopped by the church where he was baptized and grew up in the faith. And a few blocks down, I went to the bakery he used to frequent and ate one his favorite snacks: a delicious little treat called a *kremovka*. No offense to Polish people, but *kremovkas* are to Polish cuisine what life preservers are to people who can't swim: a life saver.

I took the bus to Krakow, a beautiful city where John Paul II spent many years. In the early 1940s, then-Karol Wojtyla was studying for the priesthood at an underground seminary there. During the day, he was forced to work in a factory under Nazi occupation. And not far from there was a convent he would visit regularly. It was there that he first heard about a nun named Sister Faustina who had regular apparitions of Jesus.

So Jesus appeared to Sister Faustina and revealed to her that He wanted the world to know about His Divine Mercy. Jesus specifically told her to have the vision painted with the words "Jesus, I Trust in You" at the bottom. She wasn't a painter, but she described the vision to an artist whose job it became to paint Jesus Christ's image. Talk about pressure.

But also, talk about lucky. Jesus picked her! She picked the artist. I'm jealous of everyone in the equation. Especially her.

I sat in that chapel, looking at the image of Jesus, and asked Him, "Why not me? Why not show up to me right now? You've done it before. I dare You to do it again."

That's right. I dared God. The way I'd say to a friend in the freezing cold, "I bet you can't put your tongue on that metal pole for more than a minute!" just to see if he'll do it. Sometimes I've had luck talking people into doing crazy things. I figured it wouldn't hurt to try to dare Jesus to show up to me right then and there. "I'll know for sure, without a shadow of a doubt, that You exist if You show up right now. You do want me to believe in You, don't You?"

That sounded like a veiled threat on my part. Not sure where I was going with that line of thought. I changed gears and tried to sweeten the offer to the Lord. "If you show up right now, I'll never sin again. No mortal, no venial, no sins at all. I'll live a perfectly holy life." Still no appearance.

Speaking of sweets, I had another revelation: I recalled my trip to Wadowice. "I'll even throw in a *kremovka*," I offered. Desperate times called for desperate measures. Perhaps Jesus was staying away from another Poland appearance lest He get stuck eating more pierogies, but I figured it was worth a shot. Even if the shot got shot down.

I stared and stared at that painting as if I could will the appearance to happen. It's the same thing I used to do, as a kid, after watching *Star Wars* movies. I was convinced I could have Jedi powers if I just tried hard enough. I would stare at an object, and in my head hear Obi-Wan Kenobi say, "Use the force, Lino," hoping to have the television remote lift itself off the couch and into my hand.

Turns out, I'm not a Jedi. And it also turns out God didn't want to appear to me in that convent in Poland. I was jealous of Sister Faustina— well, St. Faustina, after John Paul II canonized her—but I tried to accept God's will. And that's what makes me jealous of the saints: They didn't ask for it—or Him—but Jesus showed up, anyway.

I also think a Jesus sighting would be great for my self-esteem. I have a slightly unhealthy relationship with Facebook and Twitter and seeing how many people "like" or "follow" me. Having Jesus show up would be the ultimate like. He is the ultimate follower.

Any time an apparition has happened to someone, I think it's pretty amazing that the Lord of the Universe picked that person. His or her reward is a fast track to canonization. If Jesus—or even Mary, for that matter—decides to show up on your doorstep, you're pretty much guaranteed a ticket to heavenly glory.

Granted, while I can always find ways of being jealous of others, I also have a knack for seeing the negative in those blessings. For instance, as much as I'd like Jesus to appear to me, from then on I would always have to be on my guard—kinda freaked out that He might show up anytime, anyplace.

The doorbell would ring. I'd answer the door.

"Helloooo," Jesus would say.

"Helloooo," I'd say in return. Of course, I'd welcome Him in, and then we'd chat. Maybe He'd have an important message for me to deliver. Or, perhaps He'd just stop by to see what's new with me. Whatever doubts I might have about God would disappear because, you know, I saw God. I chatted with Him.

But what if I'm in the shower when He shows up? What if He knocks and rings the bell and I can't hear Him? What if He leaves one of those sticky notes on my front door, like the UPS guy? "Sorry I missed you! I'll make a second attempt the next time you're not available." Or, what if I'm at a bar with friends, halfway through a dirty joke, and the Lord appears? That'd be brutal.

Still, faith, it seems, would come much easier in life if we could see Jesus. If He would actually show up in person to offer His help.

There is, of course, the other negative of experiencing an apparition: People think you're nuts. Looney. Crazy. Lost it. Gonzo. Maybe just high. An apparition doesn't make for easy water-cooler talk. It's even tougher holy water-cooler talk.

"Hey, Lino, you see the Yankees game last night?" a colleague might ask.

"Nah," I reply, "Jesus stopped by the house, and I was busy writing down His message to the world for the salvation of souls. Who won?"

But for all the negatives, let me go on record—in case the Lord Almighty is reading—that I'd like You to stop by any time. It'll increase my faith, and I'll get canonized way quicker.

: CHAPTER SEVEN :
BENEDICT THE SEVENTEENTH

MY COUSIN, A MONSIGNOR IN the Vatican during the 1990s, was a friend of Cardinal Joseph Ratzinger. They weren't the kind of friends who regularly dropped by to borrow power tools or a cup of sugar, but they were close enough to enjoy a meal together on occasion. Like when my cousin invited him.

One evening my cousin invited a different cardinal friend for dinner—and since neither of them knew how to cook, that meant my Aunt Maria was asked to come to the Vatican and cook them dinner. My uncle had dropped her off at my cousin's apartment complex, and she took the elevator up to his apartment on the top floor, struggling with a heavy box of the things she'd packed to prepare the meal that night—pots and pans, cooking utensils, and all of the ingredients. The elevator opened, and in her haste my aunt tripped and spilled the entire contents of the box on the marble floor of the hallway. Pots clanged. Wooden spoons flew. Onions rolled. Who could blame her for cursing? And curse she did.

As a young woman, Aunt Maria was a celebrated opera singer. As she cursed in Italian, she didn't need to stop for a breath. Her curses hit the high and low notes, interrupted only by the sudden realization that she wasn't alone in the hallway. She looked up from trying to gather her things on the floor to face her one-man audience: Cardinal Joseph Ratzinger. He was smiling.

"Oh," she said, "Your Eminence, I'm sorry..."

He interrupted her, "Don't worry about it. Happens to all of us." (Graciously leaving it up to her to figure out whether he was referring to her clumsiness or her swearing. Or both.)

The next morning, my cousin bumped into Cardinal Ratzinger in the elevator. The future pope only had to say, with a sly smile, "I hear dinner last night was excellent," and my cousin felt compelled to hold another dinner party—the very next night. My aunt returned that night to cook another meal, this time invited to stay and enjoy the evening as a guest. Recognizing her, he simply said, "Pleasure to see you again." Classy. Cardinal Ratzinger was an equally gracious guest, complimenting my aunt's cooking.

"He's a nice man," she said matter-of-factly on the night he was elected to the papacy. To some this might seem like a thin compliment, one said in passing. Fabric softeners are nice. A soda with a straw is nice. But a pope? Nice? Yet, my aunt experienced the depth of his niceness firsthand. "I'm glad he was elected pope," she said.

To which I could only reply, "Me, too."

* * *

As a general rule, I'm rarely interested in the lives of seventy-eight-year-old German men. That is, until April 19, 2005. Up to that point, a whole generation of folks, myself included, knew only one of the 264 popes of the Church to serve as the Vicar of Christ: John Paul II. And now the Church was trying to elect a new pontiff.

It was around 5:45 in the evening on the second day of the conclave. I was eight rows from the front of the Basilica, staring at the chimney on top of the Sistine Chapel when it happened: White smoke! Wait, *was* it white smoke? The past few ballots had made it a challenge to figure out. It looked white, then gray, then back to white. The crowd around me cheered as the sputtering puffs of what might have been gray smoke were overtaken by a clear white stream. Calls of "White Smoke!" echoed in the piazza in every language.

The French contingent cried, *Fumée blanche!*

The Spaniards sang, *Humo blanco!*

Even the one Icelander present could be heard shouting, *Hvítur reykur!* (I thought he sounded like the Swedish chef from *The Muppets*.)

No doubt, that cry echoed in native tongues around the world. But I was *there*. There, amidst the laughing and singing. There, to see the tears of joy.

Thirty minutes or so later, Cardinal Jorge Medina shuffled out onto the balcony and the crowd shut its collective piehole. *"Habemus Papam!"* he said. That set us off again. We cheered. We whistled. I remember laughing at the impact of such a small statement. Yet, we were waiting for one minor detail from Cardinal Medina. Who is this pope that we *habemus*? Again, the crowd took a collective breath.

In Latin, he continued: *"Eminentissimum ac Reverendissimum Dominum, Dominum Josephum..."*

When we heard that name, we were like Renée Zellweger in that scene at the end of *Jerry Maguire*. Cardinal Medina was Tom Cruise. He had us at "Josephum." We knew by that name that our new pope was Cardinal Joseph Ratzinger, and we went wild. A Brit next to me nearly blew out my eardrums with an air horn. An air horn? Really? I can't sneak those things into a Minnesota Vikings game, yet somehow this clown had gotten it into St. Peter's Square and was able to welcome the new Holy Father as if he was the new goalie for Manchester United.

"Sanctæ Romanæ Ecclesiæ Cardinalem Ratzinger, qui sibi nomen imposuit Benedictum XVI."

Except for a bit of the *Agnus Dei* and whatever *mea culpa* means, I don't speak Latin. I was cheering like crazy, but in actuality I had no idea what name the new pope had taken. So I was grateful when an American priest standing next to me translated: "He's taken the name Benedict the Seventeenth!"

Wow. Benedict XVII. So papal!

A nerdy twentysomething American in front of us was quick to correct him. "Actually, he can't be Benedict the Seventeenth. Everyone knows the last pope named Benedict was Benedict the *Fifteenth*."

I nodded. Yes, of course, we *all* knew this. Silly priest.

"Benedict the Fifteenth reigned until 1922," he continued. "So, Ratzinger is actually Benedict the Sixteenth."

The priest who'd been corrected by the layperson shrugged. You say sixteenth, I say seventeenth. The crowd didn't care about numbers either. "Benedetto!" they cried. "Benedetto!"

Everyone was united in the same feeling: "Yes, we have a pope. But not just a pope, we have a *great* pope!" From family experience, I knew that despite the names his critics called him, we had a *nice* pope too.

Soon the cardinals were taking their places on the balconies on either side of the papal balcony, waiting for the Holy Father to make his appearance. All of us, it seemed, including these princes of the Church, were eager to see our reaction to the guy they'd voted for.

In thanks for giving us this great pope, the crowd chanted *"Grazie!"* over and over. I couldn't think of a time when I'd been prouder to be Catholic. I found myself thanking God for granting us a leader to shepherd the Church. My faith felt so real. I was a living part of our two-thousand-year-old history.

Then the curtains opened, and there he stood on the balcony: "Benedict the Seventeenth!" I yelled, to the disappointment of our nerdy American friend. "Sorry, the Sixteenth!" I corrected myself. This would take some getting used to.

I remember how he waved his arms and the genuine grin on his face at our happiness. I remember how remarkable it was that, suddenly, this friend of my family looked like a pope. I was like a teenage girl at a Justin Bieber concert, yelling and waving and chanting his name in the hopes that he would hear me. When he began to speak to the crowd in Italian, it seemed as if he was talking just to me. Here's the translation of what he said—feel free to interrupt it with cheers and applause. We sure did.

> Dear brothers and sisters, after our great Pope John Paul II, the cardinals have elected me, a simple, humble worker in the vineyard of the Lord. I am consoled by the fact that the Lord knows how to work and how to act, even with insufficient tools and I especially entrust myself to your prayers. In the joy of the Risen Lord, trustful of his permanent help, let us go forward, sure that God will help. And Mary, his most beloved mother, stands on our side. Thank you!

Our humble worker in the vineyard then prepared to give the crowds his first papal blessing. We dropped to our knees. Everyone bowed their heads. Everyone except me. No way was I going to miss seeing him give his first apostolic blessing.

That night, long after he departed from the balcony, we laughed and waved at where he'd been standing, chanting the prayer we so often cheered for John Paul II: *"Viva il Papa!"*

Over the years of Pope Benedict's papacy, I got to see him in person lots of times. His demeanor was nice, just like Aunt Maria said. He was so pleasant that he bordered on being delicate—in a good way. He had a peace about him that folks like me are intimidated by. A peace that comes from knowing God and having such a strong relationship with Him that you know *he's* on his way to sainthood. And I should follow his example.

* * *

Monday, February 11, 2013.

Hey, did you hear the pope quit?

The plan was to do my radio show live from Texas all week. Sunday night, I met up with a big group of listeners on a Catholic Guy Pub Crawl in Austin. We went from bar to bar, enjoying drinks and laughs. I didn't get back to my hotel until a little after midnight. Knowing it would be a long week of shows, I took the rare step of turning my cell phone off and decided to sleep in the next morning. I woke up around 10:30 A.M., ready to start the day. When I checked my cell, there were dozens of text messages and voicemails. As I scanned my texts, the same words kept popping up: *pope, wow, resigned.* I rubbed my eyes. The Holy Father resigned? It was stunning. Television and print media outlets wanted me to do interviews, but I wasn't sure what to say. It all was so…not papal.

I was shocked. While words like *resign* and *step aside* were used, it felt to me like he *quit.* I had some definite reservations and mixed emotions about the whole idea. Popes don't quit; popes die.

John Paul II, in the midst of suffering, wouldn't resign because "Christ didn't come down from the cross." It was a decision that I, along with others in the media, regularly defended. Eight years later, it was only natural to ask if something had changed. Did Christ, in fact, come down from the cross? Of course not. And yet, out of love for Benedict and for the Church, I had to defend his decision as one of humility and service. As I wrestled with my own emotions, I tried handling the situation with humor.

I imagined him that last night in the papal apartments, smuggling out soaps and robes like you would from a fancy hotel.

Over time, I came to better understand Benedict's XVI humble, honest, and saintly decision. And anyway, it probably works out best for me. I'm guessing if anyone asked him if he thought I should be canonized right away, he'd say, "*Nein!*"

: VENERABLE :

: CHAPTER EIGHT :

CRYBABY

"JESUS WEPT."
I've heard this is the shortest sentence in the Bible. (The fact that I'm too lazy to investigate if this is true or not—and my biblical illiteracy—probably makes Baby Jesus cry.)

Why did Jesus weep? Because He found out that His friend Lazarus was dead. And so Jesus did the most human thing possible: He cried.

Jesus then did the most divine thing possible: He brought Lazarus back from the dead. Which meant, I assume, that Jesus and Lazarus definitely became BFFs. But it also probably meant Jesus could hold that miracle over Lazarus' head any time He wanted.

Jesus: "Hey Lazarus, can you get me a cup of water?"

Lazarus: "Get it yourself. I'm kind of busy here."

Jesus: "Yeah, no problem. If it wasn't for me, your carcass would still be rotting in that tomb. But sure, I'll get the water myself."

Uncomfortable pause.

Lazarus: "OK. Here's your water." And...scene.

Nonetheless, the point is that Jesus is God. But He's also human—human to the point of tears. Christians forget that basic theological truth at our great peril. He was like us in all things but sin. Which means He cried. Which means, if we investigate further, that when we cry, we're Christlike.

I'm happy to admit I'm an emotional person. I have feelings, and I'm in touch with my emotions. Unfortunately, they are the emotions of a teenage girl with mental problems.

And yet, as a sign of solidarity with Jesus Christ's tears, I present to you a Top Ten List of Places I've Cried.

10. Confessional in Minnesota, 2000

It was a lazy Saturday afternoon. The line was short that day: one person in front of me, one person behind me. I'm sure it was just a typical summer Saturday for the priest as well. Maybe he golfed that morning, was hearing confessions in late afternoon, would celebrate Mass, followed by a relaxing evening.

And then I walked in. I had examined my conscience and was ready to recite a pretty standard laundry list of sins: some venial and some mortal. A little pride, some lust, gossip, jealousy, uncharitable thoughts. Standard fare; none of the sins were new to me. But for some reason, the gravity of my sins hit me more than ever that day.

"Bless me, Father, for I have sinned. It's been one month since my last confession..." I started welling up. By the time I was halfway through the confession, I was crying so hard I was gasping for air and breathing heavy. It must have been so uncomfortable for the priest. It's one thing if someone is gone from the Church for twenty years, returns, and weeps tears of repentance for the past, then tears of joy for the future. But I was just a random dude who hadn't been to confession in a month. Bawling my eyes out.

I know if I were on the other side of the confessional, I sure would think, *Get a grip, boy! Act like a man.*

For my penance, he asked me to read Psalm 51. When I walked out of the confessional, wiping away tears, the guy about to go in looked worried. Whatever had happened to me in there, was it going to happen to him?

I then sat in the church, reading the psalm, and I continued crying. You'd have thought I had gone through a death in the family or experienced some kind of tragic loss. Instead, I was just some person in a Catholic church crying his eyes out over sin.

9. Mount Sinai, 2012

For more than a decade, I'd wanted to visit the place where Moses received the Ten Commandments. There were challenges, however: The mountain isn't the easiest place to reach. It's all the way out in Egypt.

I flew from New York to Rome. Rome to Cairo. Cairo to Sharm el-Sheikh. Then a three-hour drive into the Sinai desert. A desert, coincidentally, which had recently been the scene of several kidnappings. I'd have to survive that as well. And that was the easy part. When I finally got there, I would have to walk three thousand steps to reach the top.

As I've gotten older, my left knee has really started to become a problem. You could call it a "trick" knee. The trick was convincing myself that said knee would be strong enough to walk up three thousand steps. In the middle of the night. Oh yeah, that's the other fun part about this: It happens in the middle of the night.

Six months before my trip, I started physical therapy. Three days a week I worked with a physical therapist on cumbersome leg exercises. My absolute least favorite exercise involved her winding a giant rubber band around my calves, and making me take long strides in the hallway. I walked like a duck. It was embarrassing. What was more embarrassing was that my legs weren't getting any stronger.

And then the day arrived. I made it to Sharm el-Sheikh, hoping for the best. At 1:30 A.M. I began my climb. After nearly four hours of a moonlit walk, I reached the summit. My legs had given me the strength to make it. (By the way, Moses must have been in excellent shape as he headed up and down that mountain.)

At the peak, I looked across the mountain range of the Sinai desert and stood where Moses once stood. This is where God gave him the Ten

Commandments. I then realized I should have brought a Bible with me in order to be able to read the full description of Moses' experience, but I wasn't heading back down to get it now.

Then the sun started peeking over the mountains. It was by far the most beautiful sunrise I'd ever seen. Watching the sunrise over the mountains, I thought of how many times I'd wanted to be here, how difficult it was to make the trip, how dangerous it was to make the trip. I thought of family members who'd never be able to see the beauty in front of me. And yet, here I was. I'd made it. And I cried masculine, physically therapeutic tears.

8. On an airplane somewhere over the Pacific Ocean watching *The Notebook*, 2005

The first time I saw this film I was on a flight home from a trip to China. The Chinese apparently censor everything but chick flicks, because I could have used a little *Crouching Tiger, Hidden Dragon* to keep from crying. And while there may have been other factors for my emotions—jet lag or altitude, let's say—the truth is *The Notebook* has plenty of plot points that make a guy cry.

Well, maybe not a guy, but definitely a girl.

That Ryan Gosling, when he's out in the rain talking about how much he loves Rachel McAdams and… What, you aren't with me? Well, if you haven't seen the movie (that is, if you are a man), I won't ruin it for you. But there's a line from James Garner—who played that macho detective on *The Rockford Files*—and his wife is suffering from dementia, and…

I discovered that, on an international flight, if you want to make the person next to you uncomfortable, break down in tears while watching a Ryan Gosling movie.

7. My bedroom, 1971–present

I think you'll give me a pass for all my tears as an infant, right? But let's jump cut to me in my late twenties and this revelation: I cry myself to sleep at night at least once a year.

It's usually out of frustration of some sort.

With God: "Lord, why do you seem to ignore my pleas for help?"

With others: "Why do they make my life so difficult, and why do I feel so alone?"

With myself: "Why are you crying like a little girl with a skinned knee?"

Sometimes it's a solitary, Native-American-in-an-environmental-commercial-style teardrop rolling down my cheek. Other times it's more cathartic.

One of my more heartfelt bedroom cries was in 2006, the night before leaving Minnesota to move to New York and take a job on the radio as "The Catholic Guy." As I said my night prayers, I asked God to protect my family and friends. And then, I thought more about my friends. Guys I grew up with, went to college with, worked in television with. They knew me better than I knew myself; they had been with me through a lot of highs and lows, and I felt like Judas betraying them for thirty pieces of NYC silver. I cried as I thought of the friends I was abandoning in my quest for fame and fortune. Through my tears and sobbing, I asked their forgiveness for being a bad friend. I thanked them for their loyalty.

Then I remembered that it was only a two-and-a-half-hour flight and I got hold of myself. I also recalled that I'd be working in Catholic radio, so fame and fortune wouldn't be an issue. Which caused me to cry again.

6. Basketball court, 2003

I used to belong to a really expensive gym, because I thought it was a good way to network with people. Plus, the gym had private individual showers for men who don't like showering with other men. Which describes me pretty accurately. Because group showers are not where I want to do my networking.

A few months into my membership, a voice called out to me from the nautilus machine.

"Lino," I heard over my headphones, which were blaring the soothing, yet motivating, sounds of Metallica as I benched the bar with five-pound weights on either side.

"Hey, Ted," I replied. He was a pretty important television executive I hoped would hire me. *Maybe this networking thing will pay off.*

"Good timing to bump into you, because we're looking to hire talent for a new project we're working on and you might be just the guy. You interested?"

"Of course!" I said in a tone that gave away my neediness.

"Great, you could meet some of the guys today if you'd like. We're playing basketball and could use another player. You any good on the court?"

I assessed my skills mentally. I think it's fair to say that if an NBA scout were judging my play, they'd probably describe me as: "A horrible passer, can't drive to the hoop, has no ability to shoot a three-pointer, but at a certain range with no defenders can occasionally make a midrange shot. If he's lucky. Sometimes."

"Yeah, Ted," I said with confidence. "Count me in."

About five minutes into the game, our side had the ball. Ted was driving to the hoop—which I determined meant I could stand around and watch—but then he decided not to take the shot. Instead, he passed the ball directly into my groin.

I dropped to the ground in pain and began to cry. For several minutes. Which caused a stoppage in play. And a stoppage in me potentially getting that job.

By the way, I quit that gym.

5. John Paul II's tomb, 2005–2011

After John Paul II died in April 2005, he was buried on the lower level of St. Peter's Basilica, in a place appropriately called the Tombs of the Popes. There are lots of popes down there, but of course no one is walking by Adrian IV's tomb and crying out, "Lord, why did you take him from us back in 1159? We miss him so much!"

I had a great devotion to John Paul II, but I had no idea how affected I'd be by visiting his tomb. Being at his funeral was emotional enough, but months later I figured I could handle visiting his tomb. I figured wrong.

I knelt down in front of his tomb and the words "I miss you" just came out. As did the tears from my eyes. And snot from my nose. "I miss you. The Church misses you." To not have his voice, his presence, in the world left such a void.

I eventually controlled myself, which was a good thing, considering thousands of tourists were passing by. And then I saw an Eastern European girl walking by. (Well, I didn't check her passport, so I have no proof that's where she was from. But the stone-washed jeans, crazy frizzed-out hair, pale skin color, jacked-up teeth, and pretty much everything else gave me a tip-off. This was someone I might have cruelly called "EuroTrash" in any other setting, to get a laugh.) But then, I saw her make the sign of the cross as she walked by his tomb—and I lost it again. To think of the impact this man had on so many people's lives. Hundreds of millions of people missed him. Not because he was a celebrity, but because he was our pope, our Papa.

4. Nassau, Bahamas, 1995

It was my first time living outside the United States. It had sounded like such an adventure: Move to Nassau, Bahamas! The weather is beautiful, the people are friendly, and they've got the catchphrase, "It's better in the Bahamas" for a reason, right?

Right.

The flight to Nassau was fine. Got my luggage and was picked up at the airport for the drive to my new place. The neighborhood was dangerous. My apartment looked more like a jail cell than living quarters for a free person. Plus, it was 90 degrees, 90 percent humidity, and my place had no air conditioning.

As I started unpacking my things, I found a book my dad had given me called *Mr. Blue*. That aptly described how I was feeling at that point. Inside, as a bookmark, was a prayer card from my mom. On the front was an image of two children near a stream of water. One child, apparently the clumsy one, was about to fall into the stream, but his guardian angel was protecting him. On the back was a note in my mom's handwriting: "May your guardian angel protect you. Love, Mom."

Cue the waterworks. And I assume my mom was saying I was a klutz.

3. Church of the Holy Sepulchre, 1999

I was with some friends, and we went into a chapel for Mass. The song during the Preparation of the Gifts (which is about the halfway point of Mass) was "Were You There When They Crucified My Lord?" From purely a logical point of view, the answer to the question should be, "No, I wasn't there. It happened nearly two thousand years ago and I hadn't been born yet."

But this time, the song hit me like no other song ever has.

"Were you there when they crucified my Lord?" I sang. And then said a quiet "yes," which caused me to start crying. Then, sobbing. I was simultaneously blowing my nose, wiping my eyes, and trying not to distract everyone else.

The song ended, the priest began talking, and I was crying so hard I could barely catch my breath.

By time we got to the Eucharistic Prayer, we all knelt down and I started getting it a bit under control. I then looked to my left, and there in the chapel was a marble column. It was the remaining piece of the column to which they had tied Jesus when they whipped Him.

Uh-oh.

My whimpering turned into weeping. Weeping to sobbing. Sobbing to full-out lamentation and wailing. Jesus was whipped and beaten while tied to that column. He died not far from where I was praying.

This lasted up through the Our Father and the Sign of Peace. "Peace be with you," I muttered through tears to the poor souls standing next to me. I was nearly inconsolable, and when my friend Don exchanged a sign of peace with me he had a look in his eyes that was part pity and part wondering, "When will it end?"

I finally got a hold of myself for Communion, nearly twenty minutes into my crying fit. Turns out I *was* there when they crucified my Lord.

2. Emmy Awards, 2002

I think it's only natural that we all seek the attention of others in one way or another. A little recognition that says, "Job well done." Whether it's being named employee of the month or the pope honoring you with a medal for a lifetime of service to the Church, it's healthy to be recognized.

When I attended the Emmy Awards in 2002, I had won back-to-back Emmys to that point. It was neat having the phrase "Emmy-award-winning" in front of my name versus what had been there before: "big-nosed freak."

Having won twice in a row made me feel like I was no longer an outsider in the business I loved so much. I finally fit in and was accepted. My talent and ability were recognized. It gave me a confidence I wasn't used to. And a confidence that would only be strengthened when I won for the third year in a row.

"And the Emmy goes to...not Lino Rulli."

OK, it wasn't phrased that way, but that's how it felt. After losing—or as one friend put it, "definitely not winning"—I told the friends I was seated next to that I'd be going to the bar. Instead, I went outside and started crying. These were tears of a person who felt like an outsider in the business he loved so much. He finally realized that he didn't fit in and wasn't accepted. His talent and ability were not recognized.

And to make matters worse, I'd have to return the tux with tear stains. Literally, the tears of a clown.

By the way, if you'd like to learn more about my first Emmy award, you can read about it in my book, *Sinner*. And if you haven't bought a copy of the book yet...

1. Me writing at my desk, right now

I'm very sad you haven't purchased *Sinner*. OK, I'll wipe away the tears. But at least that brings us to the present day.

The devil makes me think that crying is feminine. Guys tell me that, too. And most women share that sentiment. So to summarize: The only people who tell me that crying is feminine are the devil, men, and women. This, in and of itself, makes me cry. Whimper. Weep. But opening up the waterworks is the most human of emotions. In fact, it's a divine emotion. As the old saying goes: "To err is human; to cry, divine."

Wait, that isn't the old saying? Even better, I just made it up.

We need more saints who laugh, who cry, and who are fully human. And I'm fully human, seeking to be with the Divine.

: CHAPTER NINE :

SEXY COP

IN THE SUMMER OF 2001,
it was time to pretend to live like an adult. I moved into my first apartment in Minneapolis. I started thinking seriously about becoming a priest. Every month I had a one-on-one meeting with my archbishop to talk about the life of a priest: celibacy, obedience, simplicity of life, as well as the day-to-day workings of the priesthood. I really wanted to become a priest, but whether God was calling me to the priesthood was a whole other question.

One afternoon, the archbishop ended our session with what he called his biggest piece of advice. "At this point: No dating."

"With my face, Your Excellency, that shouldn't be a problem."

The archbishop laughed. Then he paused. "The self-deprecating jokes are fine, but there's a truth in the spiritual life, and it is this: When we try to follow God's will, the devil will place many obstacles in your way. If you ask God for patience, your patience will be tested. If you ask him for the gift of celibacy, that too will be tested."

"Well, I'm committed to it." I was trying to convince the both of us. No dating. No flirting. Nothing until I thoroughly discerned my vocation.

In addition to discernment, which felt like a full-time job with no pay (which is ironic, since the priesthood is like two full-time jobs with very little pay), I had lots of TV work, including a weekly appearance on the local Fox affiliate's pop-culture panel. After the show one day, a fellow panelist invited me to his Halloween party.

"You've got to come," he said.

"No, I don't. I don't really like Halloween."

He looked surprised, as if I had just said I don't like breathing air.

I explained: "Adult males shouldn't like Halloween. I'm wary of those that do. I understand women having a 'girls night out' where they get all dressed up. But I don't understand guys who want to dress up. What self-respecting adult male wants to play 'dress-up'? That's cute for little girls. Not for men."

At the end of my out-of-the-blue anti-Halloween rant, he wrote down the party information on a piece of paper. "You're coming," he said. "I own hair salons. There will be lots of girls. It'll be good for you."

Hair salons? Girls? Good for me? The archbishop had warned me about him. He was the devil in disguise, tempting me. And it was working. Only one thing stood in my way: dressing up.

"Do I have to wear a costume?" I asked.

"Yes," the devil answered. He was as confident about his Halloween party as I was that I needed to discern properly. So I came up with a perfect costume that would continue my discernment yet still work for Halloween: I'd go as a priest.

There are a couple of advantages to having the number of priest friends that I do. For example:

They can offer a sacrament in a pinch.

Free Halloween costumes.

My buddy Fr. John loaned me a black shirt and Roman collar. I had my own black pants, as I didn't want to ask a celibate male if I could wear his trousers.

The night of the party, I put on the "uniform" of a priest for the very first time. It was weird how something as simple as a black shirt and white tab collar could say so much. It meant something: a life of service. Sacrifice.

Fully giving myself to God. Few outfits off the rack at JCPenney can make that kind of statement.

I looked in the mirror. *This could be it. Maybe this is how I'll dress the rest of my life. I'm a priest.* I then made sure my hair looked good, because if the priesthood thing didn't work out I still wanted the women at this shindig to, well, shin-dig me.

On my way to the party I stopped at a gas station. After filling up my car, I went in to pay. (Hey kids, fun fact: There was a time in history where you couldn't pay at the pump with a credit card. You actually had to go into the gas station and have communication with other human beings. Weird, huh?)

I picked up a few essentials and brought them to the counter.

"Will that be it, Father?" The attendant asked, waiting for my answer.

I forgot I was wearing the collar. I looked down at the items I was buying: a six-pack of beer for the party, a tin of Altoids for the beer breath, and some beef jerky for the drive home. Quite an evening it appeared I had in store, huh? Like priests don't get enough of a bad rap.

"Yes, my son." Of course I said it. Even if I became a priest, it would be years before I'd get the chance to say that again.

It was dusk as I drove to the party. As it was the last day of October in Minnesota, the temperature was in the 50s. I decided to enjoy the warm spell and drive my Jeep Wrangler with the top down and the Beastie Boys blaring. As I pulled up to a stoplight, collar around my neck, Ad Rock, MCA, and Mike D blasting from my speakers, I'm guessing the folks in the car next to me didn't know what to make of my appearance. Was I an actual priest listening to "Hey Ladies"? Or was I just some punk dressed as a priest for Halloween?

It made me wonder if I could quiet certain aspects of my personality— like my love for the Beasties—if, in fact, I became a priest. *How much am*

I willing to sacrifice? Am I willing to have my life scrutinized? What I listen to, how fast I drive, what I eat? All because I'm serving God as a priest?

Suddenly, I felt wrong wearing the Roman collar as a costume. It symbolized too much. Even though it was just a shirt, it represented something much more. Plus, any girl I met who thought it was sexy that I was dressed as a priest needed serious psychological help. Which I would find too attractive for words.

When I parked in front of the house, I found my backup plan in the trunk (well, the little storage space considered a trunk by Jeep owners). I always kept an extra pair of jeans and a button-down shirt there just in case the night, week, or month would take me someplace where I'd need an extra change of clothes. I changed out of the priest garb and into the Lino garb before heading in.

I soon saw the party featured the standard cast of characters you'd expect at a Halloween party:

The guy dressed as a human dartboard. Clever.

The naughty nurse. How original!

The not-yet-out-of-the-closet gay guy dressed as a woman.

And then… the guy who didn't dress up, and who, when you ask him, "What are you for Halloween?" says, "Drunk."

I didn't have a story. I showed up as Lino. And some people, unfortunately, guessed my costume correctly: "Oh, are you dressed as a sad clown?"

The local weather guy from the TV station was at the party, too. He was a great guy, a real local celebrity. But if I thought the life of a priest might be difficult, hanging with him at a party made me realize how easy priests have it.

Every five minutes or so, someone would spill beer on him and demand to know tomorrow's forecast. At one point, a girl yelled from across the living room: "You didn't say it would be this cold!" As the night wore on, the drunks got aggressive: "Hey, you didn't predict that tornado that came by and blew away my trailer, you son of a…"

Just a guess, but I think the suicide rate of TV weather people is higher than, say, that of sportscasters.

My fellow pop-culture panelist found me and introduced me to the women who worked at his salons. "Lino is a Catholic," he said. "He loves the pope."

Being Catholic makes for weird introductions. He would have never said, "Meet my Jewish friend, Shlomo. He loves circumcision!" Or, "This is my Muslim friend, Mohammed. Don't draw a picture of the prophet!" But with me it's always, "Here's my Catholic friend, Lino. Isn't it wild? He looks normal, but he's *Catholic!*" My friends get the biggest kick out of introducing me as *Lino, The Practicing Catholic*, as if I'm some rare species trying to find a mate at the zoo. "Sshhh, kids. It's the rarely seen *Young Practicing Catholic*. Don't make too much noise or you'll scare the girl they brought him from the other zoo."

In this case, the other Young Practicing Catholic was dressed as a sexy cop—tight shirt, tied up at the waist to reveal an uber-flat stomach. Short shorts. Sunglasses. Police-officer hat. Short, black, bobbed hair. Basically, Erik Estrada, who should have trademarked the concept of the sexy cop in the early 80s.

"You're Catholic?" she asked.

"Yep, that's me."

"Me, too!" she exclaimed

She was as surprised as if she'd just discovered that we had the same birth mother. I wasn't sure where the conversation was supposed to go at that point. Should I ask her to name her favorite sacrament? Her least favorite pope? Should I borrow her handcuffs and restrain her until she revealed her thoughts on heresies of the fourth century?

We ended up talking most of the night, until the party wound down. Her friends wanted to go to a club, and she didn't want to go. I wasn't flirting with her, but I decided to be chivalrous and offer her a ride home.

"Where do you live?" I asked.

She seemed confused about where she lived. "Downtown Minneapolis?"

"Perfect, so do I. It's no problem to drive you home." Because chivalry is all about mileage, and my car was a lease.

We hopped into the Jeep and hit the road. We didn't say anything for the first five minutes or so. The wind was whipping around the Jeep and the Beasties were blaring.

"So my brother and I became Catholic two years ago!" she yelled. "We joined after attending RCIA."

It wasn't until my mid-twenties that I heard about RCIA (the Rite of Christian Initiation for Adults), where adults—get this—choose, of their own free will, to become Catholics! As a kid in my neighborhood you were either Catholic or Lutheran or whatever. But I had had never heard of adults changing their religion. Or choosing religion in place of none. I had always thought of religion as a birthmark. You've got it; you live with it.

"I grew up in an anti-religious home, and I've always been a rebel," she explained. Then I turned down the radio.

Things were starting to make sense. She'd become a member of a religion out of rebellion, but she'd taken rebelliousness to an all-new level. I might be willing to rebel with a haircut, but becoming Catholic as a statement against her parents? Nine months of classes, baptism, confirmation, First Communion, the Easter Vigil Mass—that's a lot of work. I gave her credit for creativity and style points.

"Yeah, we just decided to… Get off at this exit," she said.

"I'd never heard of Catholicism referred to as an 'exit.' Very existential of you."

"No, no, get off at this exit!"

She was pointing to the same exit I always used.

A mile later she directed me to take the same right I would take if I were going home. "And at the light, take a left."

"Wait," I asked, "do you live in Riverwest Apartments?"

"Yeah, how did you know?"

"That's where I live."

"Seriously?" She was positively gleeful at the prospect of us being both Catholic and neighbors.

Why had I said yes to going to that party? There I was, intentionally trying to be chaste, yet bringing a girl home from a party. With priest clothes stuffed in a bag in the trunk. We pulled up to the twenty-story building.

"Umm, should I drop you off at the front?" I asked, feeling uncertain.

"Well, I guess if you live here, you can just park, and we'll go in together."

I pulled into my parking spot, we got out of the car, and I escorted the sexy cop into our apartment building.

In the elevator, she pushed the button for floor five. I pushed sixteen. When we arrived at her floor, we shared a lame good-night elevator hug.

"Unless you'd like to invite me up?" she said with a smile.

Get off the elevator at your respective floor is what I wanted to say. Instead, not wanting to be rude, I said, "Sure, yeah, why didn't I think of that?"

In my apartment, I had nothing to offer her but a mug of water. After about fifteen minutes of witty banter, I yawned—the obvious sign that she should start clearing out.

"Can I sleep over?" she asked, the water apparently diluting none of her oddity.

"What? Why?"

"Well, I have narcolepsy. I might fall asleep on the way back to my apartment."

She must have been sent by the devil on a chastity-quashing mission. Otherwise, she made no sense.

"I'll go with you. If you fall asleep in the elevator, I'll catch you if you fall. Even better, I'll just carry you to your bedroom right now. If you doze off along the way, I'll leave you in your bed."

She was insistent: "I just think it's best if I sleep over."

What could I say? I've always struggled with the word no. "No-kay," I said "you can sleep over."

In seconds she'd taken off her cop hat and cop wig. Her fifth-floor apartment must have had the same floor plan as mine, because she walked right to my bedroom and hopped into bed.

"Are you going to join me?" She was pulling off her cop stockings.

"Umm, I'm trying not to hook up right now. I'm trying to be chaste, and the archbishop said…" I paused. Bringing up an archbishop at this point in the conversation could only lead to even more awkwardness. "I'm thinking about being a priest…and…well, anyway, it's best if I just sleep in the living room."

I kissed her on the forehead, turned out the lights, and closed my bedroom door. I sat down to watch some TV, grabbed a sheet and pillow for the couch, and was getting ready to do my night prayer when I realized that I needed my prayer book, which was trapped in my room with the narcoleptic cop. I assumed she'd be out cold by that point, but wanted to knock just to be polite. "Hey, are you aslee…?"

She answered before I could finish the question. "No, I'm awake."

Narcolepsy, huh? I bet she wouldn't have fallen asleep if she were watching a test pattern on television.

"Can I grab something?"

"Go for it!" she replied energetically.

"No, not like that."

She was clearly sent to tempt me. And I didn't realize a line like that could work. If this priesthood thing doesn't work out, hopefully I'd remember it.

Prayer book—and nothing else—in hand, I went back to the living room. I began my prayers with that familiar question to God: "Do You want me to be a priest? If so, I'll do it. But, Lord, help me understand Your will. And Your will is even more difficult to discern since there's a girl sleeping in my bed, when she presumably has a perfectly functional bed just eleven floors below. If I can't understand *her*, how can I understand *You*?"

The next morning, when my neighbor and fellow young Catholic, the cop, found me asleep on my couch, she wasn't as concerned about not disturbing me. She nudged me awake with her nightstick, we said our good-byes, and I assume she took the walk of shame (or in her case, the elevator ride of shame) home.

I returned the collar to my priest friend that afternoon, disliking Halloween more than ever, but closer than ever to discernment, too.

A saint isn't someone who has never been tested; a saint is a person who has been tested and, with God's help, has passed—or, with God's help, has gotten up the next morning and tried again.

: CHAPTER TEN :

THE EDUCATION OF A SAINT: FIVE LESSONS

GROWING UP, I WAS TAUGHT about Jesus and Catholicism in the same way that I was taught about math: Learn. This. Stuff. Even though it probably won't be useful in the future.

Memorize the Ten Commandments, the miracles of Jesus, the twelve gifts of the Holy Spirit. Then, imagine God the Father, God the Son, and God the Holy Spirit on three trains all headed for the same station. The First Person of the Holy Trinity is traveling at 60 mph, the Second is traveling at 40 mph, and the Third is traveling at 50 mph. If the Father is 30 miles from the station, the Son is 12 miles from the station, and the Holy Spirit is 40 miles from the station, who will arrive at the station first?

My real answer is another question: Who cares? Am I hoping to be a train conductor for divine beings? No. I need to learn it because if I can regurgitate this stuff, they'll get off my back and I'll be able to graduate from "learning stuff" to "living life."

This curriculum—disconnected from a practical, future application to life—persisted through grade school, junior high, high school, and college. In fact, the only useful takeaways I got from school can be summarized as five lessons. Note: If you plan to become a saint, you'd better learn this stuff…

Lesson 1: Look Like a Reader.

When I graduated from high school, my parents bought me a dictionary. I intentionally kept it in its plastic wrapping throughout all four years of college and both years of graduate school. In fact, twenty-four years later, I still have that dictionary in its original plastic. As a sign that I…that… well, actually, I have no idea why I didn't open the dictionary. Sometimes we spite ourselves to prove a point we don't even remember wanting to make. I think my point was I don't need to read or learn in order to be "smart."

And mission accomplished: This is the second book I've written. Which is twice as many books as I actually *read* up until the day I graduated from college with a degree in communications. Yep, like one of those illiterate athletes in an after-school special, I made it through grade school, junior high, high school, and college without ever reading an entire book. Unfortunately, my real-life version of the after-school special didn't include a hot cheerleader volunteering to tutor me.

It wasn't that I *couldn't* read. I simply didn't *like* reading. To get through school, I came up with a straightforward plan to look like a reader. I really mastered this in college. When a professor gave our class a reading assignment, I read a paragraph or two of the book—just enough to formulate a halfway-decent question. Then, in class, when the prof asked the inevitable, "Does anyone have any questions?" my hand would be the first to shoot up.

"Yes, Lino?" the professor would ask, happy to see someone participating.

"Yeah, I was just wondering why they call him *The Great Gatsby* when, based on what I read of him last night, clearly he isn't. In your estimation, what makes him great? Would he be considered great in our own day or does the word *great* have different connotations over time?" *Boom.* I'd asked a thoughtful question, one that would take the teacher at least half an hour to answer. As the prof explained Gatsby's greatness, we could all now zone out in peace. My fellow classmates, no doubt, wanted to canonize me back then.

Lesson 2: Plagiarism Is the Holiest Form of Flattery.
In my senior year of high school, I took a speech class, thinking it would come naturally to me since I occasionally speeched…I mean, talked.

Over the course of a year, we covered three kinds of speeches: informative, persuasive, and demonstrative, each one more boring or—in the case of the kid with the speech impediment—more painful to watch than the last. The final assignment for the year was to perform an entertaining speech. But the night before it was due, instead of outlining my speech, I turned on the TV, and there was a Rodney Dangerfield Young Comedians Special on HBO. I loved stand-up comedy, and I was hooked. That night, for the first time, I saw a young comedian do a hilarious set. His name was Jerry Seinfeld. You may have heard of him. But in the fall of 1988, Seinfeld wasn't *Seinfeld*. He was just…Seinfeld.

Hey, I thought. *He's pretty funny. Why don't I do his routine for my speech tomorrow?*

You may be thinking that stealing someone's material and pretending that it was my own would be wrong. And you'd be right. But it seemed like a win-win to me: I got to watch TV and prep my speech at the same time. Jerry would never know. And that was about as much as my moral compass could guide me back then: If I wasn't going to get caught, it couldn't really be that bad.

I took out a pen and paper and wrote out his set word-for-word. That night I practiced it more than I'd practiced any of my other speeches. My favorite joke went something like this:

"I had a parakeet that used to fly around the house and crash into these huge mirrors in my living room. Ever heard of the interior design principle that a mirror makes it seem like you have an entire other room? What kind of jerk walks up to a mirror and goes, 'Hey look, there's a whole other room in there. And there's a guy that looks just like me in there.' But the parakeet would fall for this. I'd let him out of his cage, and he'd fly across the room, right into the mirror. *Bang!* Even if he thinks the mirror is another room, you'd think he'd try to avoid hitting the other parakeet!"

I titled my speech after Jerry's signature opening line, "Did You Ever Notice…" The next day in class, I did what the assignment required me to do: I entertained. In fact, I more than entertained. I killed. My classmates wanted an encore, and I would have happily obliged, but unfortunately I'd already used up all of Jerry's material.

When I got my final grade, though, it was as if *I'd* run into a mirror that I had mistaken for another room. For the jokes that made Jerry Seinfeld a billionaire, I got a *C.* As Jerry would say, "What's up with that?"

I didn't have a well-formed conscience, so that's part of the reason I felt OK ripping Seinfeld off. If I had ever opened up that dictionary my parents bought me, I might have discovered that the word *plagiarism* comes from the Latin root meaning "to kidnap"—as in kidnapping someone's idea. I wasn't kidnapping Jerry Seinfeld, but I was taking the assignment on an unauthorized ride because it, like so many requirements in school, didn't make sense to me. Yes, it was fine for someone like me, who enjoyed performance and theater, to memorize lines and deliver a joke. But I always felt bad for the kids who weren't natural public speakers. I knew their pain because I'd experienced it in my physical education classes. We all, it seems, have our crosses to bear.

Lesson 3: Don't Call the Gym Teacher a Gym Teacher.

Gym should be called just *gym.* Not *gym class.* There's nothing to be learned in gym except that those of us who are unathletic are to be shunned.

Great, what a lesson. My least favorite season of gym was spring, when the teacher made us play coed baseball.

We were now six months into the school year, and I was a growing boy, meaning the school-issued gym uniform—a pair of polyester green shorts trimmed in yellow, and a matching green and yellow collared shirt—didn't fit me as well as it had in the fall. My former knee-length shorts were now Daisy Dukes. My broadening shoulders stretched the shirt so much that one of the numbers tore off the back. In the fall I'd been a "10." In the spring I was a "0."

Our gym teacher looked a bit like Rodney Dangerfield but, unlike the great comedian, he wasn't making jokes. Even worse, he couldn't get no respect, no respect at all. Especially not from me. I hated that he set up a hierarchy in the "class" for every game: He picked the captains and, in turn, they picked their teams.

I hope that whoever came up with the concept of picking teams is in the outermost ring of hell waiting to be chosen for a game of grinding teeth. This cruelest form of humiliation seems reserved for the unathletic. Science classes didn't divide into teams to avoid the unscientific among us. The kid who insisted that Jesus rode dinosaurs wasn't made to stand along the wall of the biology lab, waiting in vain to be chosen for a frog-dissection team. So why was it fair to do this in gym? When it came to sports, I was always picked last, or second to last—just ahead of the girl who'd sprained her ankle. This wasn't humility; it was humiliation.

Once teams were picked, the egos of future saints forever martyred, it was time to play baseball. The gym teacher graded us on the quality of our play, which, by the way, screwed with the kids who would have had a perfect 4.0 if they'd spent less time reading books and more time swinging pine. And gym "class" was in the morning, when I least felt like *not* playing baseball.

One morning, as we were playing baseball to earn a grade, I stood in the on-deck circle and watched as my team's batter, a 6'5" football-basketball-baseball star nicknamed Schwing, hit a ball so hard that, as I write this, it is still in the air. Though the two of us couldn't have been more different, he and I got along. In the dugout, just moments before, he'd predicted that he was going to make one "ride the lightning," and when he was done trotting around the bases, he gave me a high five.

"Now you do that!" he said, trying to pump me up.

For a moment, I stood, stuck in the on-deck circle, imagining what it would be like to knock one out of the park. It would be like telling a joke that got my whole team laughing. It would be greater than anything that Gatsby had ever done. It would be like...

"Lenno," the gym teacher, hollered. "You're up."

I walked up to the plate and yawned. This upset Rodney Gymteacher.

"What are you yawning for?"

"I'm tired, sir."

"Call me *Coach*. And excuse me, but is baseball boring to you?"

"You're excused. And yes, sir, it's boring."

"Coach," he insisted. "Call me *Coach*," as if he were a drill sergeant on the first day of boot camp. "What makes it boring, Rulli?"

Ahh, so he did know my name. As I considered what made baseball so boring, the pitcher threw the first pitch.

"Strike one!" the ump yelled.

"Wait, what?" I turned to the ump. Even my classmates on the opposing team thought the call was unfair. "We're actually playing here? I'm talking to the gym teacher and you..."

"Coach!" the gym teacher yelled. "Call me *Coach!*"

The pitcher threw another ball across the plate.

"Strike two!"

"Seriously?" I said to the ump. Then turned back to the gym teacher. "Why should I be graded on how I play baseball anyway? I'm not gonna be a baseball player when I grow up…"

"Not with that attitude you won't be." For him, anything in the world was possible with just a little hard work.

The pitcher threw a curve ball.

"Strike three." The ump behind the plate grinned through his mask. "You're out!"

The gym teacher could not have been more satisfied. "Go to the bench, Lenno."

I was satisfied as well. "Go to hell, Coach."

You'd think he would have been happy that I finally called him *Coach*.

Instead, I learned my first and only lesson in gym "class": Telling your gym teacher to go to a place of eternal punishment and suffering wasn't a Christian thing to do. The Christian institution I attended, however, had no problem sending me to their version of hell: Saturday detention for the rest of the school year.

Lesson 4: Demonstrate School Pride.

Here's another thing I learned in high school: How to pick a lock. There wasn't a lock-picking class per se offered by the school, but rather an extra-curricular activity sponsored by my friend Ron, an upperclassman who took me under his wing early on in my high school career. Wherever he went, Ron carried ten silver steel picks in a convenient carrying case. I remember them as the tools of one of the greatest mentors of my life.

At first, he showed me how to pick easy locks with them, like the lock to our English classroom. Our English teacher had the most foul breath of any human being on earth, and originally I thought we were breaking into her room simply to leave mints on her desk as a subtle clue. Instead, Ron picked the lock on that door simply because it was the farthest classroom from the principal's office. We were less likely to get caught down there.

After school, we met outside her door. "A lock," Ron explained "is basically a set of pins." He had a way of breaking down a problem much more effectively than my teachers. With Ron, I didn't have to take notes, and I wouldn't be tested on it later. With the pressure off, I absorbed the information like a sponge—a lock-picking sponge.

"You got it?" he asked.

"Yep, I've got it perfectly." He'd explained it so well, in fact, that if I wasn't worried about being made an accomplice in a petty crime, I could list the steps right now, here in this book.

In our free time, we'd pick locks simply for the satisfaction of opening a door without a key. Too soon, the satisfaction of simply picking locks turned into tedium. It was like needing to fry an egg and choosing the roof of a car on a hot summer day instead of a pan and a stove to get the job done. Sure, at first it was fun and all, but the novelty wore off. We wanted to fry bigger eggs.

"I've got an idea," Ron said. He'd stopped by my house one night, wearing black jeans and a matching black shirt. "Let's break into school and pull a prank."

Breaking and entering sounded enjoyable to me, and since I had yet to take a class in law enforcement or the perils of jail time, I told him to count me in. "Let me just go find some black clothes to change into," I said, ready to go.

"No, not now." Turned out, it was just laundry day and black was all Ron had to wear.

"I'll pick you up Sunday night," he said, "Don't tell anyone."

Who would I tell?

That Sunday night, we pulled up to the back of the building. Our school didn't even have an alarm system, and many of the doors were still single-bolted. We chose the weakest point of entry, the gymnasium, the unprotected fortress of one Mr. Call-Me-Coach. Within seconds, we were inside.

"Hey, Ron," I said, as we made our way, flashlights in hands, through the locker rooms and into the hallway that ran parallel with the main hall of the school, "this is kinda weird. We do everything we can to avoid school during the day…and now we're here at night on our own. Why are we here again?"

Unbeknownst to me, he had a specific prank in mind. One that had to do with the name of our school: Hill-Murray. It was so named after the merger of Hill High School and Archbishop Murray High School. At least, that's what we were told. If I'd been a reader, I might have known who those two guys were. Instead, it was just more proof to me that it is easier and more effective to simply name Catholic institutions after recognizable figures of the faith: "God High School" and "Jesus Elementary," for instance.

Ron led the way through the main section of the building. He stopped at the door of the woodshop classroom.

"Pick this lock," he said, obviously more confident about my skills than I was. "Then find some large pieces of thick cardboard and a handsaw. I'm going to the roof. I'll be back in a few minutes."

So I dutifully took out the tools of the trade and got to work. I surprised myself when I had the lock picked in under a minute. By the time he got back, I'd completed the mission.

"Be on the lookout to see if anyone's around," he said, "I need a few minutes in here."

Standing in the empty hallways of my high school, flashlight aimed into the darkness, I was proud that *something* I'd learned in school was paying off. I'd picked a lock. I was standing guard. I felt accomplished and could see that all the money my parents spent on a Catholic education was well worth it.

After a grueling twenty minutes or so, during which the only sound I heard was Ron sawing, he finally appeared with a large piece of cardboard cut into a shape that I couldn't see. He handed me a roll of duct tape. "Follow me," he whispered.

Where else could I go? I followed Ron as he climbed a quasi-secret theater-geek-only staircase to the roof. Once outside and on the roof, we hurried to the main entrance of the school. Below us were the doorways through which our fellow classmates would pass the next morning. In front of us stood the letters that, like the Hollywood sign, advertised our school's name: Hill-Murray. It was then that I noticed the shape of what Ron was carrying—a giant cardboard *B*.

"Help me out here," he said.

Together, we used the whole roll of duct tape to secure the *B* on top of the *H*. We had renamed it: Bill-Murray High School. My soon-to-be alma mater. The institution that taught me how to pick a lock.

Lesson 5: Read What You Like.

The fall of my senior year in college, I decided to see for myself if this place that some said was helpful—the place of purification called the "Career Counseling Center"—actually existed, and if there was anyone there who would be willing to "counsel" me on a "career." As I wandered the halls, I bumped into a theology professor from a class I'd taken the year before.

"Hey, Lino. What are you up to?" he asked. Finally, an authority figure who remembered my name.

"Actually, I'm looking for help in deciding what to do after I graduate." I'd liked him as a professor, and I asked him if he could help me.

"Have you ever thought about a graduate degree in theology?"

His question picked some kind of lock in my brain. Because we were at a Catholic university, I'd taken his course and one other in theology. Looking back on the classes, I remembered that I had enjoyed them. I recalled caring about the topic. And I realized that I'd never once been tempted to kidnap someone else's theological idea. I never gave a speech titled: "Did You Ever Notice…That a Lot of Prophets in the Bible Were Pooh-Poohed in Their Hometowns?" Maybe I could be the Schwing of theology. I might like the game enough to knock some theological concepts out of the park.

It dawned on me: Was bumping into this theology professor just a coincidence, or was God leading me to something? I figured that would be the type of thing I could actually learn if I took some more theology courses. And so, in a move that seemed completely out of the blue to my friends and family, I applied for—and was accepted into—a program to get my master's degree in theology.

The first book I purchased for a graduate-level class was *The Message of the Prophets*. The cover featured a picture of one of the prophets—which one, I didn't know—but I wanted to learn who that guy was. For the first time in my life, I wanted to read a book. By the time I was drafting my thesis two years later, I had read almost a hundred books. It was a miracle.

That encounter with the professor is how God usually speaks to me. It's as if He's throwing me pitches. Not wild pitches like a booming voice from the heavens telling me: "Lino, I need you to become a nun." But instead, the Lord lofts up a softball; something I can hit because my soul sees it clearly.

Until bumping into that professor, I had never, not for one second, considered theology as a major. And yet, when the opportunity presented itself, it just made sense. *Theology* made sense, because it was true.

That's what I've come to believe about God and about faith: *When you know, you know.* Over the years, I've tried so hard to discern God's will in my life. Strange as it might sound, I would have loved to have been a priest. I fought hard to make it my vocation, but if I were meant to be a priest, at some point in my life I would have connected with that pitch. I didn't.

And the other thing I've learned, although it's tough to accept, is that I'm not going to be good at everything. I should thank God if I'm good at anything! So, whereas school measures well-roundedness with grades in topics as varied as gym, science, home economics, and woodshop, I think that flies in the face of our unique, God-given strengths and talents and abilities. I didn't understand why I disliked so many of my classes in high school and college. But maybe it was so that when I took a class in theology, it *would* click. I'd be able to say, "Oh! A sign from God."

Like the saints, I've learned to let God lead me to places I never imagined I'd go. Not my will, but His be done—that's the adventure of the Christian life. That's the adventure of living a holy life.

Though, I grant you, saints rarely tell people to go to hell. I'm still working on that part.

CHAPTER ELEVEN

ARE THERE ANY SIDE EFFECTS?

I WEAR MY FEELINGS ON my sleeve. In fact, not just on my sleeve—but on my pants, shoes, undergarments, and everyplace else. My feelings control the majority of decisions in my life.

If I feel like praying, I pray. When I don't feel like praying, I don't pray. When I feel l like working out, I go to the gym. When I don't feel like it, I eat potato chips. In fact, to the great frustration of my ever-patient publisher, when I feel like writing, I write. When I don't feel like writing, I miss my manuscript deadline by two months.

And yet, when it comes to my feelings, I'm reminded of the sage wisdom a therapist told me years ago: "*Feelings* aren't facts." I'm also reminded that I said to him: "I *feel* stupid I pay you for this crap."

The first therapist I went to was fresh out of college (me, not him). Technically, he wasn't a therapist. He was an Evangelical pastor/therapist/ snake oil salesman. A nice guy with a master's degree in counseling, but he had no clue what was going on.

"Let's pray about it," was his response to everything. He always wanted to pray our way through things.

Then, like now, I wasn't the holiest guy on earth, and I never felt like prayer would be the answer to everything. I believed pretty strongly that while everything *can* be prayed for, not everything *will* be answered in prayer. If I'm hungry, and I pray real hard, God could remove my appetite or He could have someone show up with a casserole, but He usually doesn't. If I'm hungry, I have to make some food for myself. Or pay someone to make it for me. Or have my mom around. But prayer doesn't fix my hunger issue.

If I was having a problem with girls, he'd say, "Let's pray." When I had issues with a family member, he'd respond, "Let's pray." And when I didn't have enough money to pay him for his services one week, he said, "Well, let's talk about it." Somehow, when it came to money, he didn't want to pray. He just wanted me to pay.

My second therapist experience was in the mid 2000s. A friend of mine, Mike, who'd been in three-day-a-week therapy for nearly a decade, suggested I start seeing a therapist. I tried not to take it personally. And I gave him credit for bringing it up, since it's not the type of thing you can casually drop into conversation.

"Hey Lino, you watch Letterman last night? By the way, you're mental. You should really go see someone about that. Anyway, great monologue."

This therapist's name was Dr. John. He didn't like his patients referring to him by his last name, which got me thinking of my own title: I have a master's degree in theology, but I don't go around asking people to call me Master Lino. Maybe I should.

This time, seeing as he was a full-blown therapist, not just a pastor-therapist, I was hesitant to meet with him. There's a stigma attached to therapy; it's not something you want people knowing about you, even though it just means you're trying to improve yourself, which shouldn't be seen as a bad thing.

However, just as many people see confession as too public an acknowledgment that someone is a sinner, many people (including me) see those who go to therapists as weak.

Nonetheless, like most things in life, I had to take the leap of faith. I'm not getting my sins forgiven without the confessional. I'm not getting mentally healthier without therapy. Plus, Dr. John was a practicing Catholic. So he would "get" me.

In the waiting room at my first appointment, who should come out of the office but an old college classmate.

"Hey Lino! What are you doing here?" he asked, as if the answer wasn't obvious.

I thought about lying. "Oh, hey, Steve. Just here to drop my crazy friend off for therapy. He's in the car waiting patiently in a straightjacket."

Then I admitted: "I'm going to therapy." It was weird hearing the words come out of my mouth. I could only hope he wasn't judging me as harshly as I was judging him for being a total nut job who needed help.

In the coming months, I'd bump into all sorts of people I knew. Turns out Mike and I had lots of mutual friends. And he must have thought all of us needed therapy—or he got a commission for each person he sent Dr. John's way—because every time I went to therapy, it was like a reunion of sorts.

Sometimes friends were there in couple's therapy. Once I ran into an ex-girlfriend there, and I could only imagine that Dr. John was unfortunately hearing about me in two sessions back-to-back: hers and mine.

When I first met with him, his office seemed too comfortable. He had a beautiful leather couch that, I assumed, his patients were paying for. Which made me think we were paying him too much. As I sat on the couch, he stared at me. Then, softly, he asked me a question: "So what brings you here?"

In my own hushed tone, I responded, "I'm crazy," hoping for a laugh. I got nothing. I then launched into a diatribe I had rehearsed in my head a million times over.

"OK, so I'm insecure. I have a desperate need for people to like me, and at an even deeper level, I hope that they can accept me as I am."

"Go on," he whispered.

"I seek approval. From the world, from my peers, from strangers. My self-worth comes from how others see me. What they think of me. Whether they like me or not. And so, my psyche can be terribly damaged at any time. Which is a scary way to go through life."

"Go on," he said in a slightly more encouraging tone.

"The career path I've chosen, well, it's not exactly good for my insecurities. I've hosted my own TV show; I've been a TV reporter. I've worked for the major television networks. I've worked for well-known cable networks. I've even worked for PBS—granted, the check from PBS was only thanks to viewers like you…" I paused, waiting at least for a smile. I got nothing. Why I tried for another laugh line only reminded me of my insecurities. "Ratings define my worth as a person. If someone on the street asks for my autograph, I feel affirmed. I feel loved. And that's a dangerous way to live."

He paused for a moment, looking me up and down again. "So you work in television?"

Ouch. That's the last thing my ego needed.

Now I was on the defensive. "Yeah, I've been on TV since '98. Even won a couple Emmy awards," I said, trying to boost my own confidence and self-esteem.

"You know," he replied, "I do have some well-known figures that visit me. They enter through a secret side entrance near the back of the building so as not to be bothered by the public…"

I was assuming that sentence would lead to "…so let's have you come through that entrance from now on."

Instead, the sentence lead to…him rubbing in the fact that maybe if I were more successful, I'd get welcomed to that entrance. But I didn't make the cut. Which is exactly the type of thing that drives me crazy and drives me to therapy.

I'd have to explain in words a friend once used to sum me up: "I have a hole in my heart that can only be filled by the applause of strangers. And I *hate* that about myself."

"Go on," he repeated again, which really got on my nerves. I started hating myself…and started hating him.

"I love television. I love the media, in general. I think, professionally, this is where God wants me. But I get so frustrated. And mad. At myself, at the business, and even at God. So that's, basically, what brings me here: Me. And God. And work."

He thought about his answer before saying, "Maybe you should quit."

I didn't know if he meant quit praying, quit my job, or quit therapy, but I met with Dr. John every week for over a year. My angst and anger didn't disappear; the only thing that disappeared was the money from my checking account that paid for his comfortable couch.

So I realized he was right about quitting. Not quit my career, or prayer, but quit him. And so I did.

* * *

I'd been away from therapy about two years, when one unassuming Saturday I went to confession and got a rude awakening.

I think we'd all agree there are things you don't want to hear in a confessional:

"I'm recording this."

"I'm not wearing pants."

"You need professional help. Here's a card."

Based on a three-minute confession, a priest who'd never met me before determined I needed help. His hand reached around the confessional screen, seemingly breaking all seals of the sacrament, with a name and number.

On the business card was the name and address of a therapist. But not just any type of therapist; this was a psychotherapist. That word spooked me. *Psychotherapist.* Really? A physical therapist helps people with physical problems. A speech therapist helps people with speech. Which means a psychotherapist helps…yeah, great. Psychos.

On my first meeting with the therapist for psychos, he suggested putting me on an antidepressant. Correct that—antidepressants. As in two different ones, because he predicted that one simply wouldn't do the trick.

"Are there any side effects?" I asked.

He then recited a handful of side effects off the top of his head: "Sleepiness, insomnia, dizziness, talking more than usual, burning when you urinate, dry mouth, fever, hair loss, nervousness, upset stomach, diarrhea, headache, skin rash, restlessness, getting more depressed, thoughts of suicide or hurting yourself, decreased sex drive…"

"OK," I interrupted him, "but are there any *negative* side effects?"

"And you'll notice some weight gain."

Great, I thought to myself, *now I'm a psycho who's getting fat.*

The worse part was I couldn't drink alcohol with the medication. Well, I wasn't supposed to.

One night, against doctor's orders, I went to a party and had a few drinks. Around 2:00 A.M., details get a little fuzzy—antidepressants with vodka and Red Bull will do that. I overheard a guy talking to a girl about the Trevi fountain. Well, seeing as I spent my fair share of time in Rome at the Trevi, this was a topic I loved.

Somehow my love came out as aggression: "What do you know about the Trevi fountain?" I asked.

"What don't I know about it?" Maybe he was on the same medication I was, because he was equally as aggressive.

"It was built in 1735," he said, "and..."

Before he could continue, I interrupted. "Wrong! It was built in 1755. You're an idiot. A mor-on. Nice job, loser. Anything else you'd like to lie to this girl about? Maybe you've got a girlfriend back home and you're cheating on her? Maybe you've got an STD? Huh? Anything you want to tell us, tough guy?"

This rant came out of nowhere. I was increasingly angry at somebody I've never met before, all over the date the Trevi fountain was built.

"I'm gonna come over there and give you a slap." I'm not sure why I threatened him with a slap. It just seemed like the right place to start at the time. I've never hit anyone in my life, nor have I ever been in a fight. Nonetheless, I continued threatening him. "I'm gonna crush you like a cricket. I'm gonna stomp all over you. Then I'm gonna take your hair and sell it to old people for toupees."

At this point, the owner of the house came over and told me to calm down, or he was going to do something to me that sounded very painful. And physically impossible.

Realizing I couldn't go much further off the deep end, I promptly apologized. "I'm sorry, dude, I don't know what's gotten into me." And that was true, because I never used the word *dude* in a sentence that wasn't "I refuse, under any circumstances, to see the movie *Dude, Where's My Car?*"

I really didn't know what had gotten into me. Was it the medication? Was I lashing out at someone because of the pain others have caused me?

"I'm sorry," I said again, this time to the Trevi fountain guy.

Surprisingly, he accepted my apology, and within minutes we were laughing about my insane outburst. We even went online to look up when the Trevi fountain was built, and it turned out he was right. The Trevi was completed in 1735. We had another good laugh about that. Having made up and made friends, I decided it was time for me to leave. On my taxi ride home, however, my anger—once aimed at a stranger at a party—instead turned to someone I knew very well: me.

I hate myself, I started repeating. *I'm a loser. I'm nothing. My career is nothing. I'll never be respected by anyone in this business. I'm stupid. People hate me. I can't control myself. I'd be better off dead.*

This was new territory for me. Wanting to hurt others was one thing. But wanting to hurt myself? This was bad.

Maybe I should just kill myself. Get rid of this pain. I'm sick of people telling me I'm not good enough. That I'll never be good enough. Everyone is better than me and I can't stand it anymore. I started thinking of ways to kill myself.

Overdose. That was my first idea. I had some aspirin at home, but I'd probably need about a hundred pills. And I hate swallowing pills. I'd probably quit after five anyway, so that wouldn't work. Next.

Carbon monoxide poisoning came to mind. But I lived in a huge building with at least two hundred parking spots in the garage. Impossible.

My balcony seemed like the perfect solution. I lived on the sixteenth floor, with a small terrace I could jump off of. But I'm afraid of heights, so I knew I wouldn't have the courage.

As the taxi pulled up and I went into my apartment, I couldn't believe I was suicidal. Was it the meds? Was I going crazy? I began to realize I couldn't completely trust myself.

Inside my apartment, I did the only thing I could think of: I called a suicide hotline.

"Hello, thanks for calling 1-800-dontkillyourself." It was a woman on the other end. "Who am I speaking with?"

I had to come up with a name quick.

"Garage," I said. Guess I was still thinking of the car-in-the-garage technique.

"Garage is your first name or last name?" the voice asked.

"Yes, well, it's Garagelo…Garangelo…uh, friends call me Garangelo." This was going well.

"Garagelo, are you suicidal?" she asked.

"It's Garangelo. And my mind is all over the place. I think it's the medication. I'm not sure what's going on with my brain right now."

I wasn't using my real voice, lest she recognize me. It's the same technique I use in the confessional behind the screen. My voice is a cross between the serial killer from *The Silence of the Lambs* and a perverted Muppet.

"Do you need to go to an emergency room?" She sounded concerned.

"No," I said. "I don't want to go to the emergency room. I'm afraid they'd put me in a psych ward and castrate me."

"Actually, it's a lobotomy you're talking about. Castration is something completely different. And I think that's only done to animals," she said.

"Right. Yeah, sorry about that."

The conversation flowed rather naturally, to a variety of topics, and eventually I dropped my confessional voice and spoke as regular old me: Garangelo.

"I just want a way to deal with the pain of life, I guess. I don't want to die, but I don't know how to live."

She agreed with me. "I don't think you're suicidal, either. Maybe you're lonely and need someone to talk to. I'm happy to be here for you."

We talked a while longer, and I thanked her for her time. I was feeling much better.

"By the way," she said, "your voice sounds awfully familiar."

It was at this point it hit me. After being on television for years, some folks recognized me by just the sound of my voice. This might be one of those unlucky moments.

"I'm sorry to ask," she continued, "but are you on TV?"

Pause. A very awkward one.

"Umm…"

"I'm sorry, I shouldn't have asked. That was unprofessional of me."

Of course, my insecurities kicked in. Wanting to be recognized, I admitted it was me and that I used a fake name. "Yep, that's me. Do you like the show?"

"Yeah, you're really funny!" she said, unprofessionally helping my professional goals.

"Cool," I said with a smile on my face. "That makes me feel much better. Thanks for all that you do."

With that, I hung up the phone. Maybe all I needed was a little recognition. And to get off the medication.

That night, I went to God in prayer: "Why won't You fix me? Why do I have to struggle and fight the way I do? Do You not love me? Don't You care for me? I just want You to make everything all right."

I went to sleep, not surprisingly, without answers to those questions. But down deep, that Catholic chip that was implanted in my brain as a baby seems to keep me going. I fight the good fight and keep the faith. Mostly. Usually. Sometimes.

: CHAPTER TWELVE :
BUONA NOTTE, NONNO

"LINO," POPS SAID, "WE'RE GOING to your grandparents'."

I was about twelve years old, right at that age where I felt I could argue with my dad. But, ultimately, I knew he'd always get what he wanted, so off we went.

"We'll get lunch along the way," he said, which was especially disappointing because my grandparents were great cooks. As a kid, half the enticement of Sunday Mass was knowing we'd be going to Grandma and Grandpa's house afterward for lunch.

The genius of their food was in its simplicity. Pasta, pizza, all the regular staples, of course. But then there was what Grandma called "fried dough." I don't have the recipe committed to memory, but I believe it consisted of making dough and frying it. And I loved when Grandpa would create pepper sandwiches. He'd take a slice of bread, stack all sorts of peppers onto it, and top it off with another piece of bread. I think that's where he got the name "pepper sandwiches."

But since we weren't eating at their place, and I didn't have a job or a legal way of making money, that meant Pops was treating for lunch. Which meant we weren't going anywhere expensive.

"Where should we go?" he asked me, knowing our options were limited to a few fast-food places along the way. "Arby's or Burger King?"

"I'm fine with either," I answered truthfully.

To which he replied, "Let's flip a coin."

I accepted the idea, knowing where this would ultimately lead.

"I don't have a coin, do you?" he asked. I've never known my father to have change.

"Well, I've got a quarter," I said, handing him the coin.

"Heads is Arby's; tails is Burger King." Which meant we were going to Arby's. You could always tell what Pops really wanted to eat based on which restaurant was heads. If he didn't get his way on the first coin flip, we'd have to go two out of three...or five out of seven...or until he got the result he wanted.

As soon as the coin was in the air, I prayed it would land on heads. I've never been afraid to pray to God for the simplest (or strangest) things. And as a kid, it was the best prayer I had: "Please, God, heads!"

God as Divine Currency Decider is a beautiful icon I have yet to see created, but I think it should be done.

If I ever become a bishop, my episcopal motto will be a picture of my dad flipping a coin with me uttering the phrase, "Please, God, heads!"

The coin would, predictably, eventually, land on heads. Pops would then put the coin in his pocket, which meant that I, in part, would be paying for lunch after all. And off to Arby's we'd go...

* * *

My middle names are Gino and Armando. Gino, after my mother's father; Armando after my father's father. I wrote about Gino in my previous book, and I promised to write about Armando in my second book. This is my second book. So here he is...

As a kid, I'd only seen him as a retired guy who liked cooking, bocce ball, and beer. He was also a handyman. If we needed someone to build a bookshelf, or help fix the lawnmower, my grandpa was there. Best of all, the work was done for free!

When I didn't see my grandfather at work, I saw him at prayer. He went to daily Mass and prayed the rosary. But he wasn't a holier-than-thou kind of guy. Before retirement, he worked a day job at an oil refinery. When his shift was done, he and his buddies went to a bar just a few blocks from home. In a tip of the hat to Al Capone and *The Untouchables*, my grandpa and his friends were known as *The Unquenchables*. In short, they liked their booze.

Every day, around 5:00 P.M., the phone at the bar would ring.

"Christine?" The bartender would answer, presuming it was my grandmother on the other end of the line.

"Tell Armando to come home," my grandmother would say. "Dinner is ready."

With that, my grandpa would finish his beer and walk the few blocks home, fortified by the power of hops and barley to handle the loud and festive dinner with his wife and four kids.

Like many men in my grandfather's generation, he didn't talk much about fighting in World War II. He was part of the "Greatest Generation," a quiet, humble group who served their country and didn't bring it up when they came back. We see that as admirable, and rightly so.

Then again, what options did he have? Thanksgiving would have been weird, what with Grandpa at the dinner table detailing how he cut a Nazi's tongue out of his mouth and made a necklace out of it. "Who wants to eat?" Even if these guys wanted to talk, they were kind of limited in polite dinner conversation.

For the impolite realities of his life, my grandfather had his own area of the house. Long before "man caves" became fashionable, my grandpa had one of his own: It was called the basement. It was a no-man's-land—or to be specific, a no-woman's-land. Only the guys could go downstairs. The steps were steep and hazardous, more like something out of an *Indiana Jones* movie than part of a family home.

My grandpa made his own pasta, so one half of the basement was covered with dough and flour. He also made his own wine from the grapes he grew in the backyard. And at times he made his own rules, which is why I could see his illegal war booty: some rifles, something that looked like a musket, and a sword emblazoned with a swastika on the handle. It was the one weapon no one ever asked him about. My grandpa fought the Germans in Deutschland. We left the rest to our imagination.

*   *   *

Back at Arby's that day, Pops was telling stories of how little he saw of his own father when he was growing up, since Grandpa was away at war. "After your grandfather came back from the war..." my dad said, but I cut him off.

"Has Grandpa ever killed someone?" I asked.

My father's eyes darted around the restaurant. He looked almost as uncomfortable as when he'd had to pay. Then I remembered that we're Italian.

"No, I mean in war."

"Oh," he said with relief, as if the FBI were taping the conversations of the dining rooms of all the Arby's in the land, in the hopes of catching a member of La Cosa Nostra slipping up over roast beef and horsey sauce.

Even though I'd asked it, the question surprised me. I'd always known my grandpa as a loving, caring guy. No bad temper, no ill will. But it could have happened. He might have taken another human life.

My dad's answer has always stuck with me: "When a guy is pointing a gun at you, it's not like you can discuss possibilities with him. Especially when you don't even speak the same language. And the way I see it, Pa was just serving his country."

Don't ask why my father referred to his father as "Pa." He insisted on talking as if we grew up in the countryside or were the Italian version of *The Waltons*. It's like we said good night as a family. "Buona notte, Pa. Buona notte, Nonno. Buona notte, Giovann-boy."

Nonetheless, the idea of my grandpa killing someone was tough to bear. "I don't think I could do that," I said. "I don't think I could kill someone, even in war."

"Would you be a conscientious objector, Lino?" As a wannabe hippie, my dad was preparing to be proud.

I shook my head no. "I'm a pain objector. It's not my conscience that's the driving force. It's my fear of pain. Maybe I could kill someone, but I'd hate being killed back."

Pops didn't fight in Vietnam on account of what he says were his "damned flat feet." I think my family's DNA—which veered into coward territory about the same time my father's feet went flat—is why I admire the men and women of the military so much. They're like a different breed of human. Not that humans are bred, mind you. When I talk to veterans, I admire their courage and strength. It's a combination of qualities that makes them so different, it's as if I'm talking to a person from another planet.

"You're willing to fight for and defend our freedoms?" I ask, amazed. "Wow. So what do you do for sustenance? Do you enjoy drinking iced tea and eating pizza?" I ask, just to see if we have anything in common.

I'd love to be a hero, someone able to fight for his country. I wish I was courageous, and strong, and had great morals. For that matter, I wish I had a very strong jawline. It would at least make me look more courageous. A guy like me with a double chin just isn't seen as a threat. *Surrender your weapons, and then come over here and grab my extra chin!*

It's taken me a long time to accept the fact that God didn't create me to be courageous. I could be a chaplain on the frontlines, but I couldn't fight on the frontlines. I could be a journalist covering the story, but I couldn't lay down my life for the story. It's tough for me to admit this, because what's more admirable than fighting for one's country? What's more courageous than defending others? But saints are folks who learn to be aware of their strengths and weaknesses, whether they're proud of them or not.

I'm not a natural leader. But I thank God for the wonderful qualities that others have—whether it's courage, fortitude, or just having a strong jaw. Instead, I'm just me. Lino.

Well, Angelo, actually. My legal name is Angelo, which means *angel*. And I hope I don't sound too greedy when I say that I'm an angel... who wants to become a saint. Most angels don't have aspirations beyond hanging out with God in heaven and making the occasional appearance in Renaissance art. But *this angel* wants to be like St. Michael the Archangel, a badass warrior for the Lord. And while I may not be able to fight on the battlefields of war, perhaps when I'm a saint I can help in the battlefields of the comedic life. With my very own version of this prayer:

St. Michael the Archangel, defend us in battle.
St. Lino, just a regular Angel, defend us in verbal battle.
Be my protection against the wickedness and snares of the devil.
Be my protection against the wickedness and snares of bad humor.
May God rebuke him, we humbly pray;
May God rebuke bad comedy, we humbly pray;
and do thou, O Prince of the Heavenly Host, by the Divine Power of God,
and do thou, O Prince of the Heavenly Host, by the Divine Power of God,

cast into hell, Satan and all the evil spirits,
cast into the farthest reaches of basic cable, Two and a Half Men,
and all evil comedians,
who roam throughout the world seeking the ruin of souls.
who roam throughout the world seeking the ruin of comedy.
Amen.
Amen.

*   *   *

And while prayers aren't always answered the way we want, I'd be remiss if I didn't mention the best way to recap the difference between my grandfather's generation and my father's generation.

Even small children know that dialing 911 is reserved for reporting accidents, medical emergencies, or criminal activity. "Dad tripped and hit his head on the tub because Mommy is having a baby in the bathroom, and there's a bad man at the door offering me candy and a ride to the hospital. What should I do?" It's the trifecta of 911 emergencies, an operator's dream. My dad, on the other hand, thinks of 911 and its operators as a service that one calls when one needs to report things one has been subconsciously worried about for quite some time, those nagging concerns of his life that arrive at the conscious portion of his brain with the help of a drink or two.

Operator: "911: What's your emergency?"

Pops: "Yeah, hi, I've got some live hand grenades here."

He was referring to a handful of explosives from his father's WWII loot. It was 2004. That year my grandfather passed away, and my dad—perhaps nostalgically—was going through some of Grandpa's things. Among the guns and sword, Pops noticed a box of hand grenades. So he thought he'd share the good news with 911.

Operator: "Excuse me?"

Pops: "Well, when Pa was done with the war, he brought some hand grenades back with him and maybe they'll go off tonight."

This must have confused the 911 operator. Was he threatening the whole region with destruction? Was he a drunken citizen? Was he a hillbilly? Why was he calling his father "Pa"? Naturally, she erred on the safe side.

Jump-cut to the bomb disposal team closing our street off to traffic, placing a huge container next to our mailbox, and cordoning off our house. Like in the movie *The Hurt Locker,* a guy dressed in body armor guided a robot into our home. I had to call my friends up, one by one, and explain that it was as if R2-D2 had dusted himself off for the trip from Tatooine to our house, where he picked up my grandfather's grenades from the couch where Pops had set them, and then carried them out to the street and deposited them in the container.

Boom! The sound of a thousand death stars exploding signaled that the grenade situation was copacetic. And yes, the neighbors noticed. In retrospect, maybe it would have been easier if Grandpa hadn't brought the grenades or rifles back from the war. His son just didn't know what to do with the stuff. And neither would I.

CHAPTER THIRTEEN

EATING BAD MEAT

WINTERS IN MINNESOTA, FOR THE kids in my neighborhood, meant sledding. And since winters in Minnesota last from mid-September to mid-May, that's a lot of sledding.

Kids would climb to the top of the highest hill they could find and take great pleasure in sliding down. And they'd slide down that hill just as fast as they could on whatever would carry them: sleds, tires, other kids. The goal was speed.

Unfortunately we lived in the city, and the highest hill in our neighborhood ended abruptly at the base of an apartment building. So a kid could enjoy a few seconds of pure unadulterated speed and joy before realizing that the fun would end soon, because he was heading straight toward a ten-story brick building.

He would have to slam on the brakes (that is, dig his feet in the snow), try slowing down with his hands, and, if all else failed—and all else always failed—jump off at the last second and see the sled/tire/other kid slam into the wall with a thud. The poor sap who lived on the ground floor apartment would pop his head out the window and yell something profane (though after the thousandth time, his statements just became grunts and obscene gestures). The kid would then trudge back up the hill, dragging his sled/tire/other kid, ready to slide down again.

"Let's do it, Lino!" My friend John convinced me to give it a shot. There I was, eight years old, heading up the hill for my very first sledding experience.

Getting on the sled, I looked down at the hill and wished I wasn't trying this. It didn't seem like it would be fun, but now I had to go. I set off down the hill. Immediately, I was traveling faster than I liked. I didn't know how to stop, so I just rolled off the sled. It was the thousand-and-first hit against the poor sap's apartment.

John was thrilled. "Let's do it again!"

"No thanks," I replied. "I'm going home."

I realized at a young age that I don't like being out of control. I like having control of my surroundings, the people around me, my bowels. I've never understood speed freaks or people who actually enjoy being scared. I never got into zombie movies or horror movies either. I'm gonna pay you to scare me so I can stay up all night with nightmares? No thanks. I don't like being afraid.

"Be not afraid." John Paul II said this an awful lot in his pontificate. Granted, Jesus said it first. Oddly enough, though, when I heard JPII say it, I was like, "Whoa. I get what he's saying," and I presumed he came up with it himself.

It probably resonated with me because my fears tend to control me. So many of my decisions are based on what others' reactions to me might be. For instance, when I drive, I don't want to make a left turn if there's traffic behind me because it inconveniences others. It's not that I don't want to offend them. It's that I'm afraid they might get mad and honk at me—or maybe bump me like a police officer in a high-speed chase. Or I'm afraid they just won't like me for making that left turn and slowing down their day.

At work, I don't do some things I want to do, because I don't want to hear complaints from people who, ironically, I don't like to begin with. So get this: I'm afraid to offend people I don't like, because then they won't like me. Try to make logic out of that.

I think when it comes to faith, I'm oftentimes driven more by fear than I am by love. When I commit a sin, I'm afraid God is going to punish me more than I am saddened that I've offended God. My fear of hell drives a lot of my confessions. And in the confessional I'm usually more afraid of what the priest thinks about me and my sins than I am about what God thinks about me and my sins.

As I sit here, writing about things I'm afraid of, my mind is racing. So to give you a peek inside my head (scary, I know), I think it best to just write a list of things I'm afraid of. This is all off the top of my head, and I will stop writing after one minute.

Things I'm afraid of:
Failure
People not liking me
Girls calling me a loser
Super tan people
Super pale people
Plane crashes
Car crashes
Career crashes
Not having a career
Having a career
Missing out on fun
Foo Fighters not putting out another album
Having my fake tooth fall out in public
Having my fake tooth fall out in private
Getting married
Having kids
Not getting married
Not having kids
Eating bad meat

Time's up already? OK. Well, as I scan over the list, that's a pretty good description of me and my fears. It sums me up pretty well. But with a little reflection, I notice one thing that's not on the list that should be. If I can be completely honest of what I'm most afraid of, it is this:

I'm afraid none of this is real. God isn't real, heaven isn't real, and that when we die, that's it. I stay up some nights asking God if He's really there or if it's all made up. As you can imagine, it's a pretty one-sided conversation.

"God, are you there?" I ask. And I receive silence in return. "See, that's what I was afraid of."

So that's my biggest fear: that Christianity is made up. Not the most saintly of thoughts, I know, but it keeps me up at night.

Strangely, it's not that I have these thoughts in moments of desperation or despair. And down deep I believe that God really does exist. I'm just *afraid* He doesn't. Which, by the way, makes it odd the way I capitalize the *H* in He when referring to God.

To be fair to me, it's not that I spend countless hours every day asking God if He exists or not. But it's one of those nagging fears I have in the back of my mind, that same feeling you have after leaving the house and wondering if you left the iron on. It doesn't consume your day, but the fear is there.

And you know what? I should be canonized just for admitting this. I don't know if anyone else thinks or feels this way. I might be the sole member of the Christian faith who loves God—and yet some days wonders if He exists or not. So I'm keeping this chapter intentionally short, since another one of my fears is that by me admitting my fears, you might somehow lose faith. And you'll blame me!

CHAPTER FOURTEEN

DEAR DIARY

IF YOU ASK WHO MY favorite saint is—present company excluded—the answer will always be John Paul II. He's my model for holiness.

In my mind, he's a saint for all of us. You like music? He had an iPod. You like the outdoors? He loved kayaking. You like sunglasses? He got a pair from Bono.

He was a regular guy, with faults and with sins—before him, I had never even heard of a pope who went to confession. It never occurred to me that popes committed sins. And somehow, knowing that he was a sinner gave me hope.

I also loved that the Church put him on the fast track for canonization. It reminds us that not every saint lived so long ago that we only know about them because of statues or paintings. John Paul II, very likely, was the most photographed and seen person in all of human history. We saw him; we heard him; we knew him. And now he's in heaven. By canonizing him, we're saying, "Hey, you remember that guy who was alive a few years ago? Yeah, he's in heaven now." Which means heaven is real. A place that's more accessible. It says we can be saints, too.

I'd seen JPII in person hundreds of times. And as he got older, I knew the day would come when he would no longer be with us. Well, I knew he'd no longer be with me. I wasn't really concerned whether he was with you or not. Call me selfish.

Knowing the inevitable would come, I prepared the best way I knew how: by saving up frequent flyer miles for the occasion. Slowly my JPII miles accumulated, as I waited to celebrate the life of a saint who inspired me to holiness.

I never told anyone about my mile-hoarding because it seemed really morbid, the idea that I was stocking up miles for his death. But eventually, in the early 2000s, I had over a hundred thousand miles in my account. For whenever that day might come...

Friday, April 1, 2005

I woke up around 8:00 A.M., and still lying in bed, looked at my calendar. There were only two events listed: "Lunch with Morrie" and "Bill's Birthday."

Bill is a comedian, and one of the funniest guys I know. And wanting to give the appearance that I care, I decided to call him first thing in the morning (well, 8:00 A.M. is "first thing" for me), proving I'm a better friend than he is to me.

I reached for my cell phone on the nightstand and called him.

"Hello?" he answered, waiting for the inevitable song to be sung.

"Hey Bill, it's Lino. I'm not gonna sing. Happy birthday!"

"Thanks for the call. And since I can never remember when your birthday is, let me wish you a happy birthday, as well. What are you up to?"

"I just woke up," I replied, thinking he'd be impressed it's the first thing I did that day.

"Wait," he said, "are you calling me from bed?"

"Yeah, why?" I asked, soon realizing my mistake.

"This just feels wrong. Talking to you while you're in bed. It's very intimate. I better go. Thanks for the call, though."

He was right. But that obligation out of the way, I turned on the television. The news out of Rome was that John Paul II was ill. Not really news, as journalists had been predicting his death over the past weeks and months (or, in some cases, years). Though naturally concerned for someone I cared for, it didn't seem anything was imminent and I eventually headed out for lunch.

"I don't think the pope will make it through the weekend," were the words Morrie greeted me with. For some reason I took his prediction very seriously. And like any good cable-news journalist, I asked no follow-up questions nor did I ask his sources. "He'll probably die Saturday. Maybe he can make it to Sunday." Considering it was Friday, that seemed awfully soon.

After lunch, I decided to go to a Eucharistic Adoration chapel and pray for the Holy Father. Only a few minutes in prayer, I realized I needed to be there. Why else had I been stockpiling all those frequent flyer miles if not for this moment? Cutting my prayer short, I left the chapel, jumped in the car and headed home.

I turned on the television, and some reports were saying he already died. I remember a CNN graphic stating: "Vatican denies reports that Pope John Paul II has died," but the fact that the Vatican was even responding to those types of things meant the time may be near. On my television screen was a wide shot of the crowds in the piazza. I wanted to be there.

So, at about 2:00 P.M., I called Northwest Airlines to finally use my JPII miles. I needed a flight for that day: Minneapolis-St. Paul to Rome, Italy.

"There's only one seat left on the 5:00 P.M.," the woman on the other line informed me. "Otherwise, we don't have a seat till Monday."

"OK, I'll take the five," I decided.

"But sir," the agent replied, "that plane leaves in three hours. And you need to be at the airport at least two hours in advance."

"Yes, I'll be there, thank you." I was throwing clothes in my bag as I said it. I then called my mom. "I'm going to Rome in three hours, and I need a ride. Can you pick me up right now and bring me to the airport?" Three hours later I was in the air, heading to Rome.

This is when being a commitment-phobe pays off. I don't commit to many things, which means I can literally leave at the drop of a hat. (Just because someone drops a hat is not a very good reason to leave the country however.)

I had a layover in Amsterdam and as soon as I landed I looked for a television to see if the pope had lived through the night. After being in the air for eight hours, anything could have happened. Thankfully, he was still alive. *Hang on, Holy Father*, I thought to myself. *I'll be there soon!*

I landed in Rome, dropped my bags off at my aunt and uncle's home, and headed right to St. Peter's. It was mid-afternoon, and roughly seventeen hours after seeing it on my TV at home, I was standing in the piazza. I was in the crowds. And John Paul II was still alive! I felt so incredibly lucky to be there and pray for him.

Not that my prayers are all that valid, mind you, but I was just happy to be there. And I was also happy to see people much holier than I, presumably with their much more God-pleasing prayers, also praying for him. There we were, staring up at the windows of the papal apartments, wondering how he was doing. Everywhere you looked, people were praying for the Holy Father. Especially praying the rosary.

I've always had a love-hate relationship with rosaries. I own lots of them, which is supposed to prove that I love them. But I hate them, because I have a little ADD, so I don't pray them as often as I should. Like, at all.

Nonetheless, I reached into my pocket for my rosary. It was the one John Paul II had given to me. It always sat prominently on my desk—like a trophy or award—but I rarely used it for its intended purpose. But now I took the rosary out and began to pray for him.

It occurred to me that John Paul II must have prayed the Hail Mary hundreds of thousands of times in his life. And when I said the words: "Pray for us sinners, now and at the hour of our death," I knew that the hour of his death was coming soon.

Around me some American seminarians were singing in Latin. Nearby were some Italian kids who called themselves the "Papa Boys." They had basically been camped out in the piazza while JPII was sick. They were doing it because they wanted him to know he was never alone. Every once in a while, they'd chant his name in Italian: "Giovanni Paolo! Giovanni Paolo!"

I pictured the pope slipping in and out of consciousness yet always hearing the thousands of people out in the piazza praying for him, cheering for him. We wanted to be with our pope.

The sun set on the Vatican on the second day of April 2005. I remember looking at that beautiful sunset, wondering if it would be the last of his life.

Apparently, his last words before he died were for all of us whose lives he touched: *"Vi ho cercato. Voi siete venuti. Vi ringrazio."* "I looked for you. You came to me. And I thank you."

Hours after the sunset, there was a prayer service held in the piazza. And then a cardinal came up to the microphone and announced the words no one wanted to hear.

"Dearest brothers and sisters, at 21:37, our beloved Holy Father John Paul II has returned to the house of his Father. Let's pray for him."

There was silence. And tears. And then, in Italian tradition, we applauded.

That night, while leaving the square, I was filled with sadness. And I was jet-lagged. But knowing I was a part of something historic, and wanting to remember those days as best I could, I wrote as much as I could in my journal.

Ah, yes, I keep a journal. And I've been made fun of mercilessly for it. I started writing in it every Sunday evening, back in 1995 when I was in graduate school. It's just a simple spiral notebook, and I'm now on my third notebook.

To answer your questions: No, I don't begin every entry with "Dear Diary." It's not a diary. It's a man journal—a very masculine one, at that. Made out of human flesh. I write in my own blood.

OK, that's an exaggeration. But I don't journal every day, while sitting on a dock looking over a lake. I keep the man journal because I figure it will come in handy during my canonization process, since one of the steps for measuring a saint's life is a review of his or her written work.

And you should thank me for it, because I'm now opening up the pages of it to you—so you can relive the days of one of the greatest saints the Church has ever known: the death and funeral of John Paul II.

I always associated St. Peter's with John Paul II, the only pope I've ever known. Today, it was weird to be at the Vatican, with all these people, without him there. Today was the first time I was there knowing John Paul II was no longer our pope.

How many nights did I sit in the piazza, all by myself, seeing the lights of the papal apartments on? I pictured him working, or praying, or whatever he was doing. It was just cool to know he was there. In my mind, it was just me and him. Though he didn't know I was even there, of course. Looking up today, though, and knowing he was gone? Tough to believe.

The first time I saw John Paul II in this piazza was 1983. I'd seen him hundreds of times since then. Waving. Smiling. Blessing.

Now, sadly, I saw him being carried right towards us. I took 2 pictures. Then I made the sign of the cross, joining the rest of the crowd giving him a standing ovation.

It lasted 6 minutes and, quite honestly, it was an ovation that no one wanted to see end.

After JPII was carried into the basilica, we had a few more hours hanging out in the piazza before we could go inside to view the body. I grabbed my cellphone and called my mom back in the states to say hi. She said that the news reports were saying that millions of people were planning on coming to Rome to say good-bye to the pope.

Just out of curiosity, I thought I'd take a look down the street to see how the line was growing. It was already fifteen people wide, and it went back as far as I could see!. I thought to myself, for once... people want to be me.

Well, not me. But where I'm standing. I took a picture to remind myself of my good fortune. And to show off to people in the future.

Within only 10 minutes of the doors being opened, I was walking inside St. Peter's. I looked at the crowds behind me. Wow. Glad I wasn't there. Then I walked into the church to say good-bye to my friend, my hero, JPII.

People are here from absolutely every part of the world. Australia, Africa, Asia... and other places that don't start with the letter A. Some folks from a country called "Poland" too. Apparently they're pretty Catholic there. And they don't mind waiting in lines. Long lines! People are waiting 12 hours to have a few seconds to see JPII lying in state. That's faith. That's crazy.

They are better Catholics than I am. Lots more patience.

Walking down the street, I saw a poster that summed up the city's sentiments pretty well:
Rome cries for and honors her pope.

Mini memorials have sprouted up all over the city. People have been leaving flowers, handwritten notes, pictures... all from the heart. I think one little note I saw, though, sums it up best for me:
Pope John Paul II: The Best

ROMA PIANG
E SALUTA IL SUO
ROMA

W
PAPA
GIOVANNI
PAOLO II
IL
MIGLIORE

With millions of people in Rome for the funeral today, including leaders of nearly every country, I took a wild guess and figured I might not get a front row seat.
So I did the next best thing: I got a press pass. Out of 3,000 accredited journalists, I was allowed to stand on the colonnade during the funeral. Mom said maybe it was JP II already looking out for me. I couldn't have asked for a better view. I asked photogs to take pictures of me for proof I was really there at this moment in history.

It was awesome to
be there,
watching the sun
come up for this
historic day — in the
Church and the world.

The piazza was eerily empty at first.
Before I knew it,
the crowds arrived and
jammed the square.

The giant bell began to toll. John Paul II's funeral
was underway.

Words can't describe the emotions of that Mass.

I saw more than one journalist begin to tear up. It was all very emotional.

Santo Subito!

POLONY CHICAGO

At the end of the Mass, before bringing his body into the basilica to be buried, the pallbearers lifted up the casket. The crowds cheered. Our final good-bye to a great man.

"Santo Subito!" we yelled. And the crowds chanted one more time: "John Paul II, we love you!"

: BLESSED :

: CHAPTER FIFTEEN :

PATRON OF THE ARTS

ONE OF THE PROBLEMS WITH hiring a tour guide to take you through a place you've imagined visiting your whole life is that so many guides impose on your moment by insisting that you see the place through their eyes, not yours.

"This is where Jesus Christ was born," said my guide. "This exact spot. Not five feet to the left. Not five feet to the right. But right *here*."

I was amazed to be standing there. The lower level of the Church of the Nativity, in Bethlehem, is where Jesus was born. Strangely, it looks nothing like the manger scenes we see in artwork. Instead, it's just a cave with an exposed rock ceiling. Underneath a small altar, on the ground, is a silver star, signifying the spot where Jesus entered the world.

"Beautiful," I said. But that wasn't good enough for him.

"God became man. He entered our world right *here*. Not ten feet in front of you. Not ten feet behind you. But *here*." I was getting the sense that he'd once been accused of taking a pilgrim to the wrong cave.

"It's incredible," I said, trying to understand a truth too mysterious for words. Making the sign of the cross, I began to pray.

But my guide continued. "He didn't become man three inches to the left. Not three inches to the right..."

This guy was interrupting my prayer so insistently, I might as well have been back home in New York struggling to concentrate at Sunday Mass. It was good enough for me that Jesus Christ was born somewhere around where we were standing. Reading my mind perhaps, he said: "And not just somewhere around where we are standing. But right…"

"Here." I finished the sentence for him. I kissed my hand and touched the *exact* spot where Jesus Christ was born.

"Yes, yes," he said. "Very good."

As we walked out of the church, we heard three pops in the distance.

I turned to my guide. "Those are firecrackers, right?"

He shook his head. "Gunshots," he said. "Not so far away." It seems he wasn't as precise when it came to the location of flying bullets.

"Is that normal?" I asked, wondering to myself what he could say that would make me feel better about this situation.

"Yes. This is very normal."

Not that. He said it as calmly as if he were noting the local pollen count and an unusually bad allergy season for the locals.

Only later did we learn that Israeli soldiers had been shooting at suspected Palestinian terrorists *exactly* two blocks from the church.

This was the world Jesus Christ came into. In a cave, God joined the human family. So perhaps it's appropriate that when it comes to spending time with our own families every year to celebrate His birth, we engage in a volley of verbal gunfire.

When I was growing up, my parents would invite the whole Rulli family over for Christmas. Pops would put in a Mannheim Steamroller cassette and light the incense. Mom would make an incredibly dry ham with all the trimmings. On the table, candles flanked a lonely bottle of wine. The living and dining room would fill with family members and hangers-on whom I'd have to ask my mom to identify.

"You know your grandfather's brother's third son?" she'd whisper. "That's his stepdaughter."

Ah, good. Glad she could make it.

Before dinner, my dad would lead the family in prayer. It wasn't the typical "Bless us, O Lord, and these thy gifts." I didn't hear that prayer until I was in my mid-twenties, visiting a friend's by-the-script Catholic family. Pops has never lived life according to a script. Instead, he would lead us in a simple, from-the-heart prayer, thanking God for life, family, and food. Amen.

After dinner, we'd celebrate what is, to this day, one of my favorite Christmas traditions. Someone would dim the lights, we'd gather around the nativity set in the living room, and we'd listen as one of the adults read the story of Christ's birth from the Scriptures. At the words "She gave birth to her firstborn, a son," one of the kids would place the tiny plastic baby Jesus in the manger.

The tradition would be complete when we'd sing "O Holy Night" as a family. Mom had mimeographed copies of the lyrics and passed them around the hushed room so that we could join in the song. It was a nice touch.

Then it was time for the gifts to be opened. Irreverent gifts, to be sure. One year an uncle gave me a cigar cutter. I was seven. A cousin once wrapped up individual cans of beer as gifts for all the underage members of the family. And then there was the Christmas when my aunt gave me a copy of the annual *Sports Illustrated: Swimsuit Edition* with a condom tucked inside.

Over the years, our family unit has evolved and so have our traditions. My dad no longer puts up a Christmas tree. I don't mean that there isn't a Christmas tree anymore; I mean that he doesn't have to put it up. Since 2004, the tree has enjoyed a prominent place in the sitting room at the front of the house for all the neighbors to see.

The Church gives us liturgical seasons to create an ebb and flow to the spiritual life. Lent leads to Easter. Ordinary time is, well, ordinary. Advent leads to Christmas. Before the end of the Christmas season, Epiphany celebrates the manifestation of the Lord. If you're a Catholic, that's a good time for the tree to come down. But apparently Pops was busy that day. And the next day. Next thing he knew, it was June and he still hadn't gotten around to it. So he decided to keep it there all year. For all you fire-hazard experts out there: No, it's not a real tree. We gave up on those years ago when the cats ate too many needles and pooped what looked like Christmas pinecones all over the house. That's a whole other story.

Another way the Rulli family Christmas has evolved is that none of us knows who's actually going to show up from year to year. In the past, when our only forms of communication were landlines and the United States Postal Service, we had an exact head count. Nowadays, with every means of communication at our fingertips, it pleases no one to RSVP.

Then there's the cousin who brings her new boyfriend. Knowing how she goes through boyfriends, no one wants to invest time building a relationship with a stranger we'll never see again. This is the guy I usually get stuck next to. We talk about the subjects that strangers talk about at a bar—sports, girls, movies, or any subject that doesn't insinuate we'll ever meet again. In the last ten years or so, I've spent more time with these boyfriends on Christmas than I've spent with my family members. In addition, it's my job to nudge him out of the photo ops, lest we end up with random photos of people no one remembers in our Christmas pics.

Whereas we used to have a bottle of wine for the entire family, it's now become BYOB because we can't stock enough booze for these lushes without getting a liquor license.

"You're going to have *another* drink?" I'll ask my dad.

"Well, the wine isn't going to drink itself!" he replies.

Not all of the changes have been bad. A family tradition I'm very proud to say that I've instituted is the eradication of ham or turkey. We're not Plymouth Rock pilgrims. We're Italians. We eat like them now: pizza, pasta, dolce. A few years ago, my tastes made a run for the border when I decided that we should add Mexican food to the mix: burritos, soft- and hard-shell tacos, and margaritas. It turned out to be a bad way to celebrate the birth of Christ. I take the blame for that one.

That was the same Christmas my father gave himself a gift that turned out to be a gift for all of us: a life-sized painting of himself. When I walked though the front door, there it was, hanging right at the entrance of the home in all its glory. Oil on canvas with a simple wood frame. (Not an ornate gold frame, because, of course, that would be ostentatious.) Above the frame, Pops had installed a special light that shone softly upon his countenance. As I examined it from different angles, my father's eyes seemed to follow me like a painting in an episode of *Scooby Doo*.

It seems he'd become what the Church used to be: a grand patron of the arts. He commissioned a work of art for himself, of himself. When he stood next to the portrait, I was tempted to get in on this commissioning business. I wanted to commission someone to paint him standing proudly in front of his own portrait.

"So…what's the story behind this, Pops?" I asked, trying not to laugh.

"A friend of mine…"

"Hang on," I stopped him. "We should wait until the rest of the family is here. Everyone will want to know."

Sure enough, as family members burst through the front door (we don't believe in doorbells) and into the house, they began howling with laughter.

"Angelo, what the hell is that?" his sister asked.

When all of the most sarcastic Rullis had arrived, we couldn't wait any longer.

"Well, a friend of mine wanted to do this painting of me."

Right, it was his friend who wanted to do the picture, not the other way around.

"Who's the friend?" my mom asked.

"He's been my spiritual advisor for fifty years."

"Pops," I said, shouting to be heard over the laughter, "you don't have a spiritual advisor."

"He's a priest," he said, defensively.

"Which priest?" my mom asked.

"Well, he left the priesthood," he replied more cautiously. Only my dad would have a former priest as his spiritual advisor.

Again, all of us burst into laughter. For a moment I felt bad. No doubt, Pops felt like we were ganging up on him. Then again, he's the one who commissioned a former priest to paint a life-sized portrait of himself.

"Did you pose for it?" a cousin asked. We were disappointed to learn that it was based on a photograph. I can only imagine a former priest, with a palette and blank canvas, posing my father with the lovely music of Jewel playing in the background. I'd like to commission that as a painting, as well.

Pops kept up his defense. "Father Tom...well, *Tom* nowadays...got into painting over the past few years and thought I'd make a good subject."

At that point, another family member walked through the door, saw the painting, and laughed out loud. Pops knew there would be lots more explaining to do. Thankfully for him, most everyone had arrived and it was time to eat. Which meant time for grace.

Ever since I got a master's degree in theology, my dad thinks I should be the one who says grace. But I talk about religion on the air, in books, when giving talks, and basically whenever someone pays me to talk about God. "I don't do freebies," I remind him.

Besides, when he leads the prayer, it's much more fun. There's always a chance for heresy, if nothing else. Plus, Pops is a big liberal, so he tries to work in politics to zing the conservative members of the family.

"God, we thank you for Barack Obama. The Messiah has given us a new messiah," he says, sneaking a look at my very conservative uncle. "And for the blessings of no longer having Bush in office…"

"Hey, Angelo, that's not right…" someone interrupts.

That's when I jump in and defend my dad. "No one else in this family wants to lead the prayer. He gets to say what he wants."

He then begins what I lovingly refer to as the litany of liberal saints.

"John F. Kennedy, pray for us. Ted Kennedy, pray for us."

Eventually the meal is served.

One of my uncles is a Harley-riding guy, but he's gone organic on us, which means he can't eat anything that's served. Instead, he brings organic chips to snack on until he can get home and eat healthy. My favorite part of his eating habits is that he even feeds his beloved dog organic dog food.

His wife is the super-devout one in the family. Every year she shows up wearing more necklaces and saint medals than the year before. She's like Mr. T—except I can't tell if she's slumped over because of osteoporosis or if the weight of all the chains is just too much for her.

"Here," she says, handing me a few Catholic pamphlets. Most of them detail some unapproved vision of the Virgin Mary. The last one was authored by a guy in Detroit who claimed to be relaying the Virgin Mary's messages via Xerox copies. The Church doesn't approve of these, of course. Neither do I.

Instead of gently nudging the cousins (who don't regularly go to church and aren't into God) to maybe give Catholicism another chance, she opens conversations with aggressive Mr. T–like questions: "You still living in sin?" Or, "You know, I read once that folks who don't frequent the sacrament of reconciliation go to hell when they die." It's clear that she pities the fools who go to hell when they die. She does it with a smile, though. Maybe that's why no one gets turned off by her.

"Speaking of death," someone else pipes up, "when Uncle Jimmy died they did such a horrible job with him at the funeral home they had to keep sending him back."

"What, like an undercooked meal?" I say.

"Yeah. First the hair was wrong, then the color of the skin."

The topic shifts to criminals. This year I learned about the cousin who just got out of the federal pen after twenty years. We hadn't seen much of him, and now I know why. As if the entire family has ADD, the topics shift so quickly it's hard to keep track of who's saying what.

"What's with Frosty the snowman?" an aunt asks.

"What about him?"

"That's a corncob pipe, right? How is this a good role model for kids?"

"Well, it's actually just animation, and…" I try to offer, but I'm cut off.

"Smoking will kill you."

"Speaking of death, did you know I'm a great obituary writer?" a cousin asks.

"Oh, how'd you learn to do that?"

"I've done two of them."

"Where's the Bible?" It's Pops who wants to know. Mom is giving him the look that means it's time to put the baby Jesus in the manger.

"Should we read from Matthew this year?" My Aunt Judy always suggests this, which leads to the annual argument regarding whether the nativity story appears in Matthew or not.

"Sure it does!" She's always so sure. "I'll find it."

Minutes later, unable to find it (because it's not there) but not admitting defeat, she says, "Well, let's just read from Luke instead. Somebody tell me where it is in Luke."

The sarcasm oozes. "Toward the front."

I suggest that we put a bookmark at the spot, since clearly no one reads the Bible the rest of the year anyway. Aunt Judy can't start reading until we come to a consensus on where she should start and where she should stop. "Oh, and how do you pronounce *Quirinius*? Is it *QUEER-inius* or *Quir-IN-ius*?"

After five minutes of everyone flexing their ancient-name-pronunciation muscles, my mom raises her voice.

"Let's focus here," she says, reminding us all why she was a successful high-school teacher. She knows how to get immature kids in line.

My aunt finally finds where she wants to start: "While they were there, the time came for the baby to be born..."

"Can I ask a question?" That's my uncle. "Why would God want to be a baby?"

"Because everyone loves babies!" a cousin answers.

"Is Jesus really God?" another asks.

Oh, boy.

An uncle turns to me. "Lino, explain God becoming man."

The devout aunt answers for me: "It's just faith. You have to believe."

"No," I say. "It's not just blind faith. It's not magic. You don't pull Jesus out of a hat like you do a rabbit in a magic trick." This gets a laugh from some of the younger cousins.

"So did God take a leave of absence while He was on earth?" my uncle asks.

"Well, it's not..."

"I was once touched by the Holy Spirit," my aunt says.

"What's the Holy Spirit?" a cousin asks.

My mom gets us back on track again. "Can we please just finish the reading, place baby Jesus in the manger, and have dessert?"

Finally, something everyone can agree on. That, and singing "O Holy Night" afterward. A collection of voices, completely out of tune.

*   *   *

Saints come from disharmonious families. Mothers and fathers, brothers and sisters, aunts and uncles, crazy cousins, and people you aren't really sure how you're related to but nonetheless see every year during the holidays. Our families form us into who we are. And sometimes, they're what we have to overcome.

The truth is, I've got it easy. I love my family. We revel in one another's craziness. It's not a burden to be together; it's actually a lot of fun. In my quest to become a saint, I don't pretend to come from a devout and pious family. We don't pray the rosary together; we don't discuss encyclicals or various other papal documents. We're just…family.

It's a shame that we know about the prayer lives of saints who lived solitary lives, but their biographies often say nothing of interest about their families. Those aren't the saints I can relate to. And in generations to come, I don't think they're the ones the Church will be raising up as models of holiness. Instead, it'll be men and women with loony cousins, dysfunctional stepsiblings, and a revolving door of boyfriend-in-laws. To pretend that every holy man or woman isn't a product of his or her environment would be dishonest.

Jesus had a pretty dysfunctional extended family, and He turned out fine. Scan the genealogy of the Lord and you'll find criminals, prostitutes, and an assortment of folks that seem like so much fun I wish they were related to me! Jesus, no doubt, had to put up with His family for the High Holy Days of the Jewish faith. And I'm sure there was a drunken uncle annoying the Lord with a tacky joke.

The Church is a big wacky family, too. That's Christianity: saints and sinners, all a part of one community. So thank God that He came to earth—in that *exact* spot—because where would we be without families gathered for Christmas to celebrate His birth? In my case, certainly a chapter shorter in this book.

CHAPTER SIXTEEN

ST. LINO AND HIS WACKY COMPANIONS

MOST OF MY CAREER HAS been about me. At best, me and God. But a lot more of me than Him. And hardly anything about you—the saints I meet every day.

No matter what project I'm working on—television, radio, even this book—for some reason people only pay me if I make things about me. Even my publisher, when asking if I had ideas for a second book, was only interested in stories about my life. When I proposed other, more typical Catholic books—a book that would draw on my knowledge of theology, or a book on why Catholics do what we do—they said no one was interested in that. (Why others get to write those books, but not me, I'm not sure).

I guess I have some kind of "Catholic Guy" everyman quality. Perhaps my experiences speak to universal, shared struggles with faith. Still, I worry that when taken too far, this gift I have of navel-gazing for the good of my brothers and sisters might become, like my gift as a kisser, a temptation to a lust of self that disregards the real heroes of the Church in favor of me, me, me. So I'm going to make this chapter about you. Well, not *you* you. Don't expect your name here. But *you* in general.

The woman whose husband died young but she's still worshipping at church every Sunday, thanking God for His goodness to her. She's a saint.

The father who prays with his kids every night before they go to sleep. He's worked all day, he's tired, he'd rather be watching a game or drinking with his buddies than waiting for his kids to finish rambling on to the Lord. He's a saint. The little guy who gets bullied at school and yet is able to forgive those bullies. He's a saint. The girl who's not the prettiest, nor as skinny as a sickly model, but she has a smile on her face whenever you see her. She treats people with the same love and tenderness that Christ has. She's a saint.

And though I'm obviously documenting my cause for canonization in this book, I've also decided to compile a list of everyday folks whose causes for canonization should also be seriously considered. Perhaps, like the martyrs who the Vatican canonizes *en masse* as "St. So-and-So and Companions," St. Lino and the following categories of saints could be canonized together as "St. Lino and His Wacky Companions." Not mentioned by name, but still called as a graduating class to stand together and be recognized. At least you're getting canonized...

Old Woman Playing the Organ at Church

It's easy for me to criticize you, what with you sucking as a musician and all. Honestly, your skills are atrocious. It stretches the definition of the word *skills*, in fact. But God bless you, because you're doing what you can for the Church. Without you, there'd be no music at all. (Can I get an out-of-tune "Amen"?) We need music at church. You are the Church. You take whatever talents God didn't bless you with and aim them right back at us, your fellow parishioners. Your heart is in the right place, even if the notes aren't.

Creepy Guy Who Hits on Girls Before, During, and After Mass

You love God with all your heart and you want so badly to get married and procreate. That's awesome. But unfortunately, you see church as a meat market. You take a run at every woman that comes through the turn-stiles at Mass, and then they leave the parish because of the uncomfortable environment you've created. And I know from experience: I, too, own a carpeted van. I can relate.

Have I ever genuflected toward the tabernacle and seen a beautiful woman, been tempted to follow her out of the church, put her in a gunny-sack, bring her home, chain her to my radiator, and ask if she'd like to have dinner with me? Of course. Who hasn't? It's all for love. But it's not the right thing to do.

You deserve canonization because all you want is to celebrate the marital embrace and start a family. In your own creepy way, you're a living witness to the sacramental bond of matrimony. You'll make a fine companion…if not with a woman, at least as part of my Wacky Companions.

Parents Who Name Their Kid Jesus

I know this idea may be offensive, because in some countries and cultures the name "Hey-sus" (as I hear it pronounced) is pretty popular. Well, if I may be the ugly American—or at least, an ugly Italian American—let me say: Knock it off. I don't see how this is helpful, for a kid to be named after the Lord.

First of all, it's too much pressure to live up to. Name your kid after a crazy uncle. Or after a less-popular Bible character (Nimrod comes to mind). Name your kid after me, a saint. Give him something he can strive for, because at least with the saints you always know they weren't perfect. But naming your kid after Jesus? He can only fall short.

The main advantage, I grant you, is that I'm sure it's very affirming to hear millions of people say, "Jesus is King" or, "I love Jesus."

It'd be great to hear people yelling, "I love Lino," wherever I go—and seeing "Lino is my homeboy" T-shirts would be cool. But then I'd be filled with the sin of pride. And if I found out that they don't really love *me,* and it turned out that this "Lino" character was actually their Lord and Savior? It'd be a huge letdown.

In a world of fiercely guarded corporate names and logos, Paul wrote that God the Father gave Christ Jesus "the name that is above every name" (Philippians 2:9). Let the Lord have the naming rights.

Person Who Wants to Hold Hands During the Our Father

I know the priest says "brothers and sisters" a lot during Mass. And the Our Father begins with an "our," which gives us a sense of family. But it doesn't mean we should actually hold hands.

Now, if there's a twenty-some-year-old woman who insists on holding my hand during a prayer, so be it. Thy will be done. But other than that, no thanks.

It's bizarre to me when some guy I've never met before extends his hand before we pray. Like I want to grab a clammy man-hand while trying to recite the words.

For your efforts to remind us, in a very germy way, that we're all a family of believers, enjoy your canonization. I look forward to not holding your hand in heaven.

Person Who Gives Me a Smudge Instead of a Cross on Ash Wednesday

Fat thumbs. Lack of artistic ability. Conveyer-belt mentality. No excuses. This is the one day of the year when I announce to the world, "I am a Catholic. I believe that I am dust and to dust I shall return." Instead, thanks to Michelthumbalo, I've got a smudge. It looks like I may have been working in the garage and brushed my hand against my forehead at some point. If you don't know how to apply a cross, a task most second-graders can accomplish, we have a problem. Though I think you should spend a great deal of time in purgatory until you perfect the art of making the sign of the cross, that's up to God.

By the way, if any liturgical company would like to create an Ash Wednesday grid I would be very grateful. Something you could place on the person's forehead, and the minister of ash would simply place the ashes inside. It would be a perfect cross every time. You and your company would all be canonized with us.

Ex-Girlfriends' Husbands

When I look at ex-girlfriends on Facebook (seriously, what else is Facebook for?), I live in regret. Primarily because nearly every ex-girlfriend, or girl I went on a date or two with, has gotten increasingly more beautiful with age. Which really annoys me. They're married, they're more gorgeous than ever, their kids are cute, and their husbands are tools.

You're the greatest testimony to commitment there is in our world. You were lucky enough to get this woman to fall for your loser-self (sorry, I'm a little bitter here), and you were smart enough to realize you hit the jackpot and made a lifetime commitment. Good for you, I'll be very annoyed if my exes show up at our canonization to see you and not me. I will, however, "like" the photos on Facebook.

Guy Who Desperately Wants to Keep Talking to You about Anything

Oh, how I wish the *Catechism of the Catholic Church* covered not just the faith, but elements of social etiquette, too. This guy is one of the reasons why the Church has to spell everything out for people. Because he's lost otherwise. He spends a lot of time in parking lots while you're trying to get into your car. You've got the keys out. Ten minutes in, you hit the button to unlock the doors. Five minutes later, you're auto-starting the car. You've got the radio on. You're in. Seatbelt is buckled. GPS is saying, "Leave long talker and proceed straight." Yet he's still talking about something he heard in the homily.

Militant Hippie Girl

She's very healthy, very into nature and spirituality. To say she's a liberal insults liberals. She's so far to the left that if she goes any farther she's to the right. She kind of smells like almonds, and you expect her to be anti-Catholic. She's easily offended by the slightest slip of the tongue. "I'd like to make a broad generalization," you say. And she replies, "The word *broad* is a sexist word that holds women down!" And yet, her passion and lack of regular bathing is intriguing enough to want her to be canonized.

Super-Devout, Holy, Pious Young Priest

We get it. You're holy and well-formed. You've read several blogs about how the parish wants good, holy, faithful priests. Make a bow during the Creed? Great. But you'll pull a back muscle trying to touch your forehead to the ground. Same goes with striking your breast during the *mea culpa*. No need to Mike Tyson yourself with body blows. We get it. *Through your fault. Through your fault.* Ouch. *Through your most painfully grievous fault.* You're pious. God bless you, St. Overzealous of the Suburbs. *Pax vobiscum!* (And yes, I did the Latin just for you.)

Chastity Speakers Who Are Unattractive

You see an unattractive chastity speaker talk about "saving myself for marriage" and you think to yourself, "Well, let's be honest: What were your options?" No one will be all that interested in you, looking like that. Did you make a choice for chastity, or do you just have a lack of opportunities?

If I travel the globe telling people why I chose not to be a linebacker in the NFL, it's gonna start coming off a little hollow when I don't have the size, talent, or ability in the first place.

The difference between an ugly person not having sex and a good-looking person not having sex is that a good-looking person has options. I think we need a little more honesty from our not-so-hot chastity friends.

Chastity Speakers Who Are Attractive

You're worse than the ugly ones. You used to have sex, but now you don't? Hey, you're just rubbing it in. You constantly remind us with your good looks of the sacrifice you made. You hooked up with everyone and their cousin, then "came back to God" and are saving yourself for marriage. In other words, you had your fun and now are at peace with God. You had your cake and are eating it, too. And yet, surprisingly, not gaining weight from the calories.

Oh, and by the way, we're in a Church that isn't supposed to glamorize outer beauty. It's inner beauty that counts. So your fans are even worse. No one likes a good-looking saint, because that means you've got it all.

OK, so I've changed my mind. I'm not canonizing you. No need for beautiful saints in my graduating class. You'll take the attention away from me, which makes for a bad companion. Sorry, no dice.

The rest of you...enjoy the canonization ceremony!

CHAPTER SEVENTEEN

MY CONSCIENCE IS THE ONLY THING I'M EXAMINING

I PRAY IN THE NUDE.

Let me make several disclaimers: I'm not a nudist. I don't play naked volleyball or barbecue *au naturel*. I don't read in the nude. I'm not trying to make a statement. Though if that were the case, it would certainly be a short statement.

I'm a nude prayer because I'm a nude sleeper.

The Church gives us lots of options for prayer—intercessory, adoration, petition—yet when it comes to the topic of proper attire for private prayer She is strangely silent. Tracksuit? Cosby sweater? Anything, as long as it's enhanced by the Bedazzler? Unlike our earthly mothers who might nag us about how we're dressed, our Holy Mother offers no advice on this topic. In my research, I haven't come across any popes who have written encyclicals on the proper attire for prayer. The Vatican has failed to issue a document stating that the one who prays nude will be excommunicated.

And so it goes like this: Before bedtime, I go to the bathroom to wash up. Because I'm a germaphobe, I wash my arms up to the elbow. I scrub up like a doctor heading into surgery. And after I'm clean, I take my clothes off, get under the covers, and then I pray.

Could I, in theory, pray in my living room, then wash up, get naked, and go to sleep? Yes. But then my last action of the day wouldn't be prayer. It would be getting naked. Not a very saintly thing to do.

My night prayer begins simply with the sign of the cross and the words: "God, come to my assistance. Lord, make haste to help me." Oftentimes, I make an examination of conscience. Like most of the exams that I took in school, I don't do so hot. And yes, just to be clear, when I'm in bed nude, my conscience is the *only* thing I'm examining.

So I examine my conscience to see where I've failed God, neighbor, and myself. I think of specific examples: "I gossiped about so-and-so. Lord, forgive me for that sin." I'd tell God the story, especially if it's a good enough one that I gossiped about it, but He knows everything. So I move on.

"I spoke boastfully of myself, and for the sin of pride, forgive me." I then usually think of whatever accomplishment caused me to sin and am, once again, filled with pride.

And if there's anything else to add, like "Oh, and another thing, I shouldn't have killed that guy," I make sure to apologize for that, as well.

The examination of conscience isn't just beating myself up, though. Instead of focusing only on how I've failed, I take time to consider how, with God's grace, I've succeeded—especially in areas where I've sinned in the past. "Lord, thank you for giving me the grace not to gossip about that person." It's rare, but sometimes I can even tell Him thank you for giving me the strength not to boast of my own successes. "Oh, and another thing, I didn't kill that guy who annoyed me. Thanks for giving me the strength for that, too!"

I try not to break my arm patting myself on the back, but I also believe that the Christian life—and growth in holiness—is about small, gradual steps. The closer to God I try to get, the more of a sinner I realize I am. But I also need to acknowledge the times I've gone the way of virtue instead of vice, and notice the progress I've made.

My prayer usually ends with: "May the all-powerful Lord grant us a restful night and a peaceful death." Or I pass out. Whichever comes first.

Here's the key I've found with prayer: routine. I may change up my method of prayer. Sometimes I use a prayer book, sometimes I do a little improv prayer and work out new material, sometimes I use *lectio divina*, which is basically a holy reading of the Bible. I mix it up because even though I need a routine, I like variety. Whatever method I use, the last thing I do before I sleep is pray. And sometimes I even fall asleep while praying. I'm very holy.

As soon as I wake up, I pray. I make the sign of the cross, usually utter a groan that the day is about to begin, and ask for strength to handle whatever comes along. As I get older, my bladder is usually calling my name as much as I'm calling upon the name of the Lord. Thus, my morning prayer is often cut short by the need to visit the men's room. (Yes, I call it a men's room even in my own home because it gives the idea that someday, *someday*, there will be a woman living with me who asks to use the ladies' room.) And I do all of this while naked.

Sleeping in the nude is something that came to me later in life. Perhaps it's hereditary, because my dad is also a nude sleeper. In truth, Pops was a bit of a nude walker, as well. But only when we didn't have guests visiting. When I was a kid and my friends would sleep over, Pops would always walk around in a robe, so it was no big deal.

The summer after my college graduation, several years before I was a nude sleeper, my dad and I—along with two of my close friends from college—went on a trip through Europe. You may be wondering why my mom didn't join us on this trip. Let me reiterate: It was me, two college buddies, and my dad. Mom was smart enough not to join that mess.

Traveling with Pops basically meant there weren't just three broke guys, but four, traveling all over Europe. Our first night in Paris we stayed in a hotel whose brochure advertised itself as "just outside of the city center." In fact, it was so far out of the city I think we were in Germany. Naturally, the four of us shared a room.

"I'm going to take a shower," Pops said after a long day. I turned on the TV, and to no one's surprise, there was a Jerry Lewis film marathon. But a few minutes later, to everyone's great surprise, Pops came out of the bathroom with just a washcloth in front of his little Angelo.

I've never seen three guys—who weren't French—so fascinated by Jerry Lewis. No one said a word. We just stared quietly at the movie (which, by the way, I think is the appropriate reaction to a Jerry Lewis film even if your dad isn't nude next to you). Unfortunately, my peripheral vision being what it is, I saw Pops remove the washcloth and hop into bed. He was now naked in a hotel room with my college friends. Pops sleeping in the nude at home was one thing. But I had no idea the policy applied out of the country, as well. The next day, at breakfast, Wade had only one thing to say about it: "So your dad sleeps naked, huh?"

That, of course, was *not* the motivation for me to sleep naked.

In 2003, my friend David got married. It was a beautiful wedding in the woods of northern Wisconsin. I shared one of the cabins with another friend, Karl. We had worked together at a TV station for a couple years, and although we weren't best friends, we were certainly more than acquaintances. Upon dropping our things off in the room, he dropped one other piece of information on me: "I sleep in the nude."

I was horrified. "You can't sleep clothed for the two nights while we're sharing a room?" I asked, a bit confused.

He said he couldn't. Since he'd spent his whole adult life sleeping in his birthday suit, sleeping in anything more would be like sleeping in an actual suit.

And so, after the groom's dinner (which, by the way, was a fully clothed affair), when we went back into the room and got ready for bed, Karl stuck to his promise.

"My policy, Lino, is 'lights off, pants off.'"

He got into his bed, turned off the lights, and announced what he was up to. "Yep, I'm taking them off now!" He was nude. Or at least he said he was nude. I have no idea. It was disturbing.

But I could hear in the sound of his voice that he had a passion for his nakedness. It seemed to really bring him joy. I wanted the happiness that he, seemingly, had.

That's not surprising, of course, because I'm always chasing after happiness and joy. One thing that's encouraged me to become a better Catholic is when I see Catholics who are happy and radiant because of the faith. I want what they've got.

So, in this case, Karl's enthusiastic embrace of nude sleeping made me want to give it a try. And, at the risk of raising a new generation of nude sleepers, I have to tell you—I love it! These days I wouldn't have it any other way. It now seems so restricting and prudish to sleep with clothing on. Granted, I'm open to the whole pajamas scene if it's the kind of pajamas that look like a suit. The pants have pleats in them, and the top is basically a velvety suit jacket. That's pretty sweet. Otherwise, why go with a T-shirt and shorts when I can go the way God created me?

Besides, as a Catholic, I'm not supposed to have a puritanical sense of the human body. Sure, after Adam and Eve ate from the tree, thus sticking us with original sin (thanks again for that one, guys!), they realized they were naked. When God went to find them, they felt ashamed of their nakedness. Yet, as the Church tries to remind us, at least in theology if not in practice, the body is beautiful. God has created me and there should be no shame about my body. (Granted, when I look at my nude form in a full-length mirror, I'm not always thrilled at what I see. I just have to hit the gym more often and will feel less shame.)

My passion for sleeping in the nude hasn't blinded me to the fact that there are pitfalls, of course, to this habit.

If I die in my sleep, whoever finds me will see me naked. Which, I'm sure, will bum them out. But I'm also hoping not to die in my sleep. I don't think the whole thing is as peaceful as everyone suspects. I have a feeling I'd wake up, think, *Oh crap, I'm dying!* and then die. But I'd be in that groggy sleep-disorientation thing, which isn't how I want to go out.

I want to be one of those holy and pious saints, who, knowing they are going to die, says something profound. And I've already decided that I'd like my last words to be, "Lord Jesus Christ, have mercy on me, a sinner." However, now that I think about it, if I say, "Have mercy on me, a saint," it might boost my chances for canonization. Though on my deathbed, I won't be naked.

My preference to sleep in the nude also has its drawbacks when I travel. Unlike Pops, when I'm in a hotel room, in a foreign bed, I never sleep nude. Two words: *bed bugs.* But there are nights when just out of habit, I get naked and fall asleep. Three words: *bed bugs bite.* And the more naked I am, the more they have to work with. Which also bites.

I'm not advocating going to Mass or Eucharistic Adoration in the nude. I don't pray in the nude out of disrespect. Jesus said that if your left hand causes you to sin, cut it off. It's better to enter heaven without a hand than go to hell with both hands. And I say if what you're wearing is causing you to be distracted, take it off. Better to be naked in heaven than fully clothed in hell. I pray in the nude because it's the one way I guarantee I'm going to pray.

I don't think about my nudity, by the way, when I'm praying. I think about God and holy stuff. Which is a key element of prayer: forgetting one's surroundings. When what I'm wearing, or the stresses of the day, or whatever else is going on in my life can be dropped for a period of time, and I can be in union with God—that's the goal of the Christian life. To be with God in heaven forever.

And have you ever stopped to think about what we'll be wearing in heaven? In art, it seems the souls in heaven have two options for clothing:

1. Nothing
2. Robes

I don't own a robe, so unless we're each issued one at heaven check-in (and I highly doubt that's one of St. Peter's jobs at the Pearly Gates), I'm either going in wearing a T-shirt, jeans, and my Adidas—or I'm going in naked.

We will be there, for all eternity, seeing God "face to face." We will be with the Holy Trinity, all the angels and saints, and hopefully our loved ones. And what we're wearing will be up to God. But in case we're nude up there, I'll be ready to worship Him naked. I already do that every day.

: Chapter Eighteen :
The Lord Is My Night-Light

In college, my roommate Chris and I were the kind of friends who could communicate complex concepts using key words that we emphasized in a way that meant something only to us. When one of us wasn't being a friend, or was in some way letting the other down, we didn't have to say anything but *friend* to indicate our disappointment. Sometimes we said it even if the other really wasn't being a bad friend, but we just felt like giving each other a hard time.

And so, my junior year, I, Chris, and three other friends lived in a duplex off campus. It was our first time living away from the dorms. There were five guys on one side of the house; another group of our friends lived on the other side. This was well before I'd ever thought of myself as The Catholic Guy. We were all pretty much The Average Catholic Guys. We didn't go to church that often, probably about twice a month, even though Mass for students was Sunday nights at 9:00 P.M. The university knew its student body: "You're going to get black-out drunk on Saturday night, so we can't expect you to make it Sunday morning or even Sunday evening at 5:00 P.M. But if you could make it to church before you go to sleep—or at least head back to the bar—we'd appreciate it."

I don't think any of the five of us had well-formed consciences when it came to the faith. I doubt a single one of us believed it was a mortal sin to miss Mass. We probably thought that was some holdover teaching from the 50s or 60s, but, like the language of Mass, it had changed after Vatican

II. Sometimes we'd make the 9:00 P.M. Mass; sometimes we wouldn't. When we did manage to make it to Mass, we showed up late and sat in the front because we thought that the nice girls in church might see us as good Catholic boys.

Two of my roommates were ladies' men. Another guy wasn't great with women, but he managed to snag a girlfriend nonetheless. And then there was me and my buddy Chris. We weren't ladies' men. We were ladies' *friends*. We regularly got trapped in the friend zone and could not find our way out. We weren't the guys that girls wanted to meet at a house party and go home with. We were the guys with the shoulders that girls wanted to cry on because of the guy at the house party they regretted going home with the night before.

St. John's offered something they called "J-Term." This was a mini-mester between the fall and spring semesters when a guy could take a class in a subject he'd always wanted to explore, but didn't have time for in his normal schedule. That January, I signed up for partying and sleeping in.

One morning, my roommate Paul shook me awake. "Lino, get up!" he yelled at me, not allowing me to ease into this uncomfortable personal alarm clock. I hate the feeling of being woken up. I'd been sleeping face-down in a pool of my own drool on the couch in our living room, not having made it upstairs to my bed the night before. Clearly it was a rough night.

"What is it?" I asked, clearing my eyes and still groggy.

Paul was holding a notebook—Chris' notebook. He'd left it on the kitchen table. Inside were good-bye notes written to each of us. All of them basically said the same thing: "This isn't your fault. You've been good friends to me. Don't feel guilty."

They seemed like suicide notes. The thing was, he didn't actually use the word *suicide*. Maybe he meant he was moving out. Going back home to live with his parents. Maybe he was going on the lam. As we read them again, though, they sure seemed an awful lot like suicide notes. We didn't know what to do, as we hadn't yet mastered problem-solving skills. We started calling around to different friends' homes. We didn't want to tell them why we were looking for him. "Have you seen Chris? Did he stay over? No. OK, thanks, see ya."

As my roommates kept calling friends, the thought occurred to me to look outside.

"Should we check the garage?" It seemed like a good idea, though no one wanted to look, afraid of what we'd find.

I headed out the front door and went to the garage, pausing before opening it. I can still feel how cold the handle of that door was. At the time, I hoped it was a sign that meant no one had used the garage for a while. "God," I prayed, "Please let me find Chris." But at the same time, I was horrified that God would help me find him in there, dead. I revised the prayer. "God, please don't let me find Chris, or let me find him in here, alive." I yanked the door open, and looked around. Two old couches, some sporting equipment, but no Chris.

Back in the house, we waited. One hour turned into two. We had called everyone we knew to call, but weren't sure what to do next. Then the phone rang. "Are you guys still looking for Chris?" A girl we knew had spotted him at the library.

We piled into my car. On the way, our relief-fueled laughter was interrupted by a nagging question: "He wrote good-bye notes to go the library?"

In the parking lot, we saw his green Oldsmobile and pulled up next to it. Sure enough, he was in the back of the library, reading a book.

We pelted him with questions. "Where have you been? Why are you here? What are you doing?" He merely shrugged, as if going missing for a day was nothing. "I don't know," he said. "I'm just reading."

He came back home with us, and things went back to normal. Nobody wanted to address what had happened. I wasn't sure what questions I would ask even if I did. That night, Chris found me in the kitchen making a grilled cheese sandwich. We had plans to go out later, and I wanted to get something heavy in my stomach. Like a sleepwalker, he watched me make the grilled cheese. He seemed so mesmerized that I offered him one.

"Nah," he said. "I'll eat at the bar tonight."

"You know, we were worried about you." I felt that something needed to be said.

The question seemed to wake him up for a moment. "Lino, you didn't really think I'd do *that*, did you?" He was looking me right in my eyes.

I didn't say anything. I wasn't sure.

A week went by without the topic being brought up again. One Saturday night, we went to a house party. Chris and my roommates were all there, and I was having unheard-of luck flirting with Lisa, a girl I'd been hitting on for years. This particular night she suggested that we go back to her place. Even better, she didn't want to cry on my shoulder. Before leaving the party, I whisper-announced my good news to all my buddies, including Chris.

"Hey, I'm going home with Lisa. See ya tomorrow."

I expected him to congratulate me, but instead he looked at me and said, "Friend."

It could have meant anything. Maybe he wanted out of the party. Maybe he wanted a ride back to our place. Maybe he was tired of talking to whomever he was talking to. All I knew was that I wasn't worried about being a friend. I was hoping to become a boyfriend. And I was gone.

The next morning, after making it home, I laid on the couch all day. And I mean *all day*. I didn't leave the couch once. That night, I decided to give my liver a break by staying away from the bars. Even though it was a Sunday, I didn't make it to church, either.

When I finally turned the TV off and went up to my bedroom to sleep, I found that I was suddenly afraid of the dark. I couldn't explain why or how. But I had a bad feeling. And something told me that I should pray for Chris. I could sense that something was not right. I was scared. Scared of the dark, or scared of something else.

Monday morning rolled around, and I went to class. That afternoon in the cafeteria, somebody came up to the table where two of my roommates and I were eating. They wanted to know if we'd seen Chris.

None of us had.

"I haven't seen him since Saturday, when I went home with Lisa," I said, trying to crowbar in my good luck, which I was still reveling in.

It wasn't all that uncommon to go for a day or two without the roommates seeing each other. He might be at another friend's house. Still, my experience the night before had put me on edge. I decided to drive over to the library. Maybe I'd find him there again.

As I pulled up to the parking lot, I could see that I was in luck. His Oldsmobile was parked near where it had been parked before. I laughed. In ten minutes I'd be calling my friends, telling them that all was well. We'd be feeling that same adrenalin rush we'd all felt the week before. That night we'd goof on him for being at the library again.

I parked in the spot to the right of his Oldsmobile, and before even getting out of my own car, I could see the keys in the ignition. *Talk about absentminded. Good thing I'm here, Chris.* I decided to grab the keys. In a few minutes, when I found him in the library, I would dangle them in front of him as proof that I was a good friend. It would be one more thing I could make fun of him for. As I got out of my car and approached his, I saw him lying across the long bench seat. His feet were stretched out near the steering wheel, and his head was near the passenger door. He looked comfortable enough. Still, it was January in

Minnesota. The temperature had to be below freezing.

I needed to wake him up, but I knew, from personal experience, that a friend would do so carefully. There's nothing worse than waking someone up from peaceful slumber. So I tapped on the window. Once. Twice. No reaction. I tapped harder. Still nothing. I decided to open the passenger door quietly, figuring he'd wake up at the sound of my voice.

"Hey Chris," I said. "Wake up."

Still nothing.

I knelt down, to get a little closer, so that I wouldn't have to raise my voice. His eyes were closed. But there was blood coming from his nose. A small pool of it was drying on the front seat. As soon as I saw it, I closed the door. I wasn't sure what to do. I looked around for help, but no one was there. It was a gray, overcast day. I felt very alone. I *was* very alone. I looked up to the sky and said out loud: "God, where are you?"

No answer.

Then I went inside the nearest building, found a phone and dialed the number for campus security. A woman answered, and I could think of nothing to say to her but the truth: "I think my friend is dead."

"Say that again?" She sounded as shocked to hear those words as I was to say them. Maybe that's why she told me to go back outside and wait. In the freezing cold. Where I would be alone again. Alone and trying to make sense of what I'd just said. *My friend is dead.* Looking up to heaven, I asked again: "God, where are you?"

Soon, campus security found me. The police and paramedics followed right behind them. They taped off the area. I was still unclear what was going on. I knew, intellectually, that he must have killed himself. But I couldn't bring myself to accept it. I was later told that there was a gun on the floor of the vehicle. I never saw it, or I blocked it out. I never even knew that Chris had a gun.

One of the cops put me in a squad car to warm up and took down my statement. I don't remember my answers. I only remember wondering why we didn't ask Chris more about that notebook. There were obvious warning signs, and we ignored them. I wasn't a friend the last night I saw him.

I looked out the window of the squad car just as the paramedics took his body, set it on a stretcher, and rolled him over to an ambulance. Minutes later, the ambulance drove Chris' body away. A tow truck took his car away. Shortly after, one of the policemen gave me a phone number to call if he could be of any help, and then everyone was gone.

"God," I said again, still staring up at the sky, "Where are you?"

I drove the few blocks back to our duplex, wanting to tell my room-mates what had happened, but no one was there either. As I started to walk down towards Chris' room in the basement, I felt that same sense of fear that I had experienced the night before. As I reached the final step, the furnace kicked on. The loud noise freaked me out, and I ran out of the house like a character in a horror movie. Suddenly, I was supersensitive.

That night, all of us tried to sort out what had happened. I was less afraid with everyone around. Other friends came over to offer their condolences. Some of the girls brought food. Some of the guys stopped by with booze. Eventually, we did what was familiar to us: We went to the bar. We talked, we laughed, we hugged, and we cried. After the bar closed, we went back to the house, but I was too afraid to go to my bedroom. Drunk as I was, I was even more afraid of the dark. Before I could go to sleep, I turned on every light in the house, and then I passed out in front of the TV.

The next morning I woke up on the couch, the TV still on from the night before. Eric Clapton's music video "Tears in Heaven" was playing on MTV. Eric wanted to know if I would know his name if I saw him in heaven. I'm hungover, the morning after my roommate commits suicide, and I wake up to this? Thanks, Eric.

The days and weeks that followed were a combination of anger, sorrow, and fear. I would wake up almost every morning crying over Chris' death. Wondering what I—what we—should have done differently. What we could have done to prevent it. In his letters to us, he'd said we shouldn't feel guilty, right? That there was nothing we could have done. It seemed he'd been trying to keep us out of his mess. Still, I'm the one who discovered him. I'm the one who hated darkness. I'm the one who needed alcohol—or, if that wasn't enough, NyQuil—to fall asleep.

* * *

In 1996, five years after Chris' death, when I was living in Nassau, I was still afraid of the dark. I was twenty-four years old, and I couldn't get through the night without some sort of night-light.

Out of the blue, one of my colleagues invited me to go on a three-day retreat. The theme of the retreat was "The Lord Is My Light and My Salvation." Though I was reluctant about spending a weekend camped out in a church instead of on the beach, I decided to go. That Friday night, I arrived at the retreat center. Above the entrance, someone had strung a banner proclaiming, once again, the theme of the retreat: "The Lord Is My Light and My Salvation." *Am I supposed to know where that line is from?* I wondered to myself. *It's probably from the Bible or something.*

After check-in, the two dozen or so retreat attendees met for an icebreaker, followed by a presentation from a chastity speaker whose job it was to kill any connections we'd just made by reminding us that we weren't there to get to know one another too well. That night, I went to sleep—alone—except for the night-light that I'd packed in advance. I was determined to make the weekend about God, not girls.

Saturday morning began with Mass. Then a priest gave a talk about Psalm 27, the source of the heavy-handed retreat theme. After lunch, there were more speakers, a chance for confession, and quiet time in the evening. Before going to sleep that night, I read the Bible in bed. Not Psalm 27, but instead, verses from Matthew 11:28–29 that a priest had mentioned in one of the talks. "Come to me, all you who labor and are burdened, and I will give you rest. Take my yoke upon you and learn from me, for I am meek and humble of heart; and you will find rest for yourselves." It had brought me peace, and I wanted to reflect on it more. Tomorrow, that is. I needed that rest which the Bible was talking about. I turned off the lamp on the nightstand and went to sleep.

The next morning, we gathered for Sunday Mass, and afterward sat in a big circle so we could share with each other what we had gotten out of the retreat. What could I say? It was just a few days' retreat; a nice getaway, but I felt they wanted more. Maybe I'd tell them how I didn't know what the theme of the retreat meant. Maybe I'd tell them about being too tired to read the Bible. That's when I realized that I had slept the previous night without a light on. As small a gesture as that might seem to them, I had a story.

When it was my turn, I was ready. I talked about Chris' death, about my inability to sleep, and that the night before was the first time in years that I hadn't been afraid of the dark.

I ended my retreat story by echoing the theme of the retreat, proving I was paying attention: "Jesus Christ truly is my light and my salvation. This retreat helped me to trust God." I paused for a moment and felt sorry for the sucker who had to follow me. Try to top that story, and try to top this result: "Now I won't be afraid of the dark." Girls were crying. Men were envious.

I like to imagine what Chris would have thought of my performance. Whether he would recognize his friend Lino. Whether he'd think it was funny that I used his story as part of a faith-sharing circle on the last day of a Catholic retreat. I like to imagine him teasing me, telling me that I sounded like a Catholic evangelist embarking on a tour. Asking me if I planned to hawk an extended CD-version of my "The Lord Is My Night-Light" story. I like to imagine him mocking my voice as I delivered my final, inspirational message to the group: "Yes, the Lord Jesus Christ intervened in my life and He will in yours, too!" I'm pretty sure he'd be a good *friend* and make sure to give me grief about it.

The truth is, it's not like I broke an addiction. Nor was I freed from the bonds of lust or pride or some other sin. Instead, the Good Lord gave me the simple gift of behaving like an adult male who is not afraid of the dark. Oh, and He helped me save money on my electric bill.

And, if nothing else, once my canonization comes along, I could at least be the patron saint for kids—and adults—who are afraid of the dark! I've been there. I know what it's like. And I'll help you get over it…with God's help.

CHAPTER NINETEEN

DO IT YOURSELF

THERE ARE TWO TYPES OF people: *Do-It-Yourself* types and *Have-Someone-Else-Do-It-For-You* types.

I fall into the latter category. Which is why I don't even own a ladder. Nor do I own anything that would mean I might have to do things myself. In fact, I'm having someone type this chapter for me as I lounge on a couch with a midget feeding me grapes. Oh, I'm sorry, in case that term isn't politically correct anymore, let me rephrase that. The midget is feeding me some non-climacteric fruits that grow on the perennial and deciduous woody vines of the genus *Vitis*.

As I began working on this chapter, I decided to find out what the #1 Do-It-Yourself project might be. Of course, I turned to Google for the answer. I didn't get one, but I learned a valuable lesson: Don't type the phrase "do it yourself" into a Google image search.

Do-It-Yourselfers take too much pride in doing it themselves. You put that futon together yourself? Congrats. But let's take a look at what it really means to say you did it yourself. Here's a quick checklist for you. (Feel free to do *this* yourself, as well.)

☐ I went out to the forest and picked the tree (or, rather, trees) that would become the frame of my futon.

☐ I walked there, since I was unable to build my own vehicle. And doing things myself means not having the assistance of strangers, so I didn't ask for a ride.

☐ I assembled my own chainsaw.

☐ Since I don't know how to do that myself, what I actually did was find a loose piece of wood that kind of resembles a handle, and then I spent weeks sharpening some iron to affix to it to create a makeshift ax.

☐ After spending days cutting trees down, scrambling away just in time so that the falling trees wouldn't land on my do-it-myself self, I dragged each tree home.

☐ I made a hammer. I forged my own screws.

☐ With nothing but my intuition, I put it all together.

Voilà! You just made a futon yourself. Now, let's look back at that list. If you checked off more than one of those boxes, there's one more box to check:

☐ I'm a liar.

OK, so nobody is a total do-it-yourselfer. If you're willing to admit you're more like someone who can read the instructions and wants to establish some misplaced pride in doing it yourself, now we're getting somewhere.

My friend Tom is the ultimate do-it-yourselfer. A few years ago, he decided to turn his unfinished basement into a superior man cave. Flat-screen TV, pool table, dartboard. Being the man that he is, he also wanted to do it on the cheap. By himself. So does that mean he built the TV? The pool table? The dartboard? Of course not. He just wanted to do the wiring by himself.

I remember when he told me he was going to do all the electrical work on his own. I also remember each time he electrocuted himself and went flying across the room. That's when I really love Do-It-Yourselfers. And why I love the fact that I'm a Not-Do-It-Myselfer.

Case in point: I enjoy eating apples. But I hate biting into them. And I hate knives. So how great is it that I can go to the supermarket and buy sliced apples? Pre-sliced apples! How many thousands of stitches have been applied in emergency rooms throughout the world because some hapless do-it-yourselfer insisted that he or she knew how to slice apples better than the professional apple slicer. Just think of the arrogance!

Additionally, at a time when unemployment is high, I'm providing people with jobs. That's right, when I purchase a pre-sliced apple, I'm paying more money for this service. The company is paying someone to slice the apple. Or at least to operate the machine that slices the apple. Which means that someone has a job because I refuse to be a Do-It-Myselfer. Which means I'm helping stimulate the economy.

Also, in case it didn't occur to you, I have kept those jobs right here in the USA. (U-S-A! U-S-A!)

You would think my absolute dependence on others would most obviously apply to God. Which means you apparently have not been reading this book but, instead, just happened to land on this page.

As a future saint, I'm proud to say that I don't do anything by myself. That's because, like Jesus says in John 15:5, "Apart from me, you can do nothing." Take that, Do-It-Yourselfers! Your insistence on doing things yourselves is totally unbiblical. You're going against the Bible. Enjoy hell. Say hi to Hitler for me.

Apart from God, I can do nothing. And yet, there are things in my life that I feel occur without God's help. Putting gel in my hair, for instance. Although it's true that, as an Italian, this could be a two-man job, I do it on my own. This is something Christ rarely helps me with.

I often feel as though I dust on my own. It seems the Lord is not a fan of the Swiffer. Also, He rarely seems to appear when I say, "I'll do the dishes. You clean the bathroom." So I feel like I'm doing things without God's help a lot of times.

Thus, becoming a saint balances out two opposing truths for me:

Accepting that I'm totally reliant on God for everything and that I can't do anything without Him.

At the same time, accepting that a lot of days I *feel* like I'm doing everything without Him. Because apparently God doesn't like dusting or taking out the garbage. So I'm on my own.

I'm constantly told I can do nothing without God, and that even faith is a gift from God. But I also know I can't lie in bed all day and put my spiritual life on cruise control, simply waiting for the Mass to come to me.

Nope, becoming a saint takes a lot of work. So, while I can't do anything without Him, He also expects me to do lots of the heavy lifting.

And so I'm left with perseverance. Persevering in the spiritual life: That's why I should be a saint. That's why we all deserve to be canonized. Because we keep trying.

To persevere as a Catholic who regularly sins, however, is tougher than it looks. There are days I think I'd be better off quitting Christianity because I'm not very good at it, like when I find myself in a state of sin.

I've committed some real mortal sins as a Bible-believing, churchgoing Catholic. Enough to say to myself: "Honestly, Lino, you're not a very good Christian. You can't claim to believe in God and His commandments yet commit those sins. The two are just not compatible."

And I agree with me when I say that. Granted, it's me agreeing with myself, which sounds arrogant. Maybe even crazy. But usually the crazy people on the subway *argue* with themselves. That's how I know I'm not crazy: I don't argue with me; I agree with me.

They are sins I don't want to say out loud in the confessional. Sins that, quite frankly, my publisher would ask me to remove if I tried to print them here. Not because they're crimes, but because they're just too graphic.

What I know with certainty is this: When I'm in a state of sin, there's an emptiness in my soul. When I'm in a state of grace, I'm much more at peace.

So why do I sin in the first place, knowing it always leads to emptiness? I guess because it feels good. And because I'm stupid.

We like our sinners to sin, then convert, and then never sin again. What about a guy like me? I've met popes; I've worked in Catholic media for fifteen years. And at some point during every one of those fifteen years I've committed mortal sins. Sins that have separated me from God. And I've felt like an enormous hypocrite. So much so that I ask myself, once again, "Are you sure you're Catholic? Maybe you should quit trying."

Yet I return. To God, to the confessional, acknowledging that it's easier to quit than to stay. It's easier to give up than persevere. I set myself up for failure by even trying. But there's no way I'm not trying. So, I can't do anything without God. Yet, because I get in my own way, I can barely do anything right with Him.

That's Christianity. That's the Gospel. That's what saints are made of. Seriously, can we canonize me already?

I'll end this chapter by quoting Archbishop Fulton Sheen. Primarily because, like George Costanza before me, I want to hit a high note and walk out.

"Man could not be independent of God any more than a ray of sunlight could be independent of the sun."

: CHAPTER TWENTY :
THAT IS *NOT* THE FUTURE

HEY, YOU HEARD THE POPE quit, right? After getting over the shock of Pope Benedict XVI's resignation, there was intense speculation as to who the next successor of St. Peter would be. Some asked if it was time for a cardinal from South America. Or a cardinal from North America. Maybe a cardinal from Africa? For some reason, when folks asked if it was "time for a black pope," it felt slightly racist to me. It's one thing to vote for a guy based on his cultural background. But it's a whole other thing to vote based on his skin color. I had a tough time believing one cardinal would say to another, "I'm tired of Whitey. Let's go with a black pope!"

Behind the scenes, news organizations got busy putting together poster boards with the names and faces of the front-runners, the cardinals to be on the lookout for. They looked like the FBI Most Wanted Posters that hang in the post office. The press—of which, I'm proud to be a part—kept bringing up the same names. Cardinal Angelo Scola, of Italy; Cardinal Marc Oulette, of Canada; Cardinal Peter Turkson, of Ghana.

On the top of my Most Wanted list was Cardinal Timothy Dolan, Archbishop of New York. In addition to hosting a radio show on The Catholic Channel—a channel that he oversees—His Eminence had also recently hired me as his personal media advisor. In fact, it was a job he created just for me. *How cool would it be*, I thought, *if he became pope?* I'd be personal media advisor to the Vicar of Christ! Not to mention the fact that he could preside over my joint beatification-canonization ceremony.

Cardinal Dolan is known for his no-nonsense efficiency. Why do a beatification, then wait a couple years for my canonization, when my holiness is so clear? Especially since he would be the one personally vouching for my sanctity?

At any rate, the world's attention was focused once again on Rome. For the weeks leading up to the conclave, blowhards like myself were on the air several hours a day pontificating about what we would like to see in a pontificate.

Like his campaign manager, I phrased the needs of the Church in terms that only Dolan could fulfill. "Reform of the Curia," I demanded. "Dolan's your guy!"

"A young, vibrant leader," I suggested. "Dolan's your guy!"

"Someone whose last name rhymes with *Molan*," I offered, when nothing else came to mind. "Dolan's your guy!"

His Eminence, of course, really doesn't like to hear that kind of talk. If you want to annoy him, ask if he's going to become pope someday.

My support was genuine and well-informed, however. I work for the man, so I may seem biased and as though I'm saying this just to keep my job, but every time I see him, I like him more and more. His sincerity, his kindness, his humor, his love for people, and his love for God—it's all real. It's all there in a way that strengthens my faith. I know of no Church leader in America who has the ability to be so attractive to so many people. In my heart, I truly believed the universal Church could have used the shot in the arm that Cardinal Dolan would have provided as pope.

Day after day, the cardinals met in the congregations. After each of these private meetings, nothing was announced. "They haven't even voted on when they'll begin to vote," I joked. After making this joke for more than a week, I arrived in Rome. It was March 8, the day they announced the conclave would start the following Tuesday.

The conclave began with the cardinals processing into the Sistine Chapel. And along with my colleague Fr. Dave Dwyer, we were covering it for The Catholic Channel live from the Vatican Radio studios. And as I watched our monitor, it dawned on me how many cardinals I recognized.

In 2005, I had familial familiarity with Cardinal Ratzinger, although I didn't know him personally, nor had I met any of the other cardinals who were voting.

This time around it was different. I knew many of them. I even considered some of them friends. Certainly guys I could have a drink and a laugh with. And these were the men who were tasked with choosing the next successor of St Peter. In fact, one of them would *become* the next successor. Though I didn't share it on the air, I paused to reflect how much trust God puts in us weak human beings.

The Church is the Bride of Christ, but she continues to work on her marriage through the work (and votes) of fragile creatures like us. Scary.

The master of ceremonies announced *"Extras Omnes"*—meaning everyone but those voting had to get out. The doors closed dramatically. It was time for the voting. And, in my case, time for stalling.

We would be broadcasting live, hour after hour, until we had a pope. And seeing how long it took the cardinals to decide when they would vote on when they'd start voting for the next pope, I figured we'd be here a while. At least a week. Maybe more. I was just hoping we'd be done by Labor Day.

On the air, we would break down some of the cardinals name by name, along with their background and experience, and I'd offer my thoughts on whether they'd become pope or not. When the name Jorge Maria Bergoglio was mentioned, I didn't take him seriously as a candidate. The rumors were that he'd come in second place to Ratzinger in the 2005 conclave. And, as always, my prognostication was spot-on:

Of the information that leaked out after the 2005 conclave, there were two prominent names: Ratzinger and Bergoglio. Each of them gained traction. But, of course, Ratzinger won. Bergoglio is a bridesmaid, but never a bride.

My analysis continued by pointing out that one of Bergoglio's brother Jesuits was quoted as saying, "He never smiles." To which I could only say, And that's *not* what we want. That is *not* the future.

Words to remember: Bergoglio is not the future. But I wasn't done yet. Another thing going against him would be his age. He was born in 1936. I've never been great with math but you start to think to yourself, *Ooooh, a guy in his seventies. Didn't we just elect a pope at seventy-eight who had to retire because of age?*

In my prognostication, I was like a GPS, noting the correct route for Holy Mother Church. Helping her avoid traffic and toll roads, I wrapped up my prediction:

He's too old; that's not the direction the Church is headed. He couldn't win eight years ago. He was too old. And he doesn't smile.

It was just past 7:00 P.M. on March 13. We'd been broadcasting for four hours by that point. A steady drizzle of cold rain drenched the folks waiting in the square for smoke. Whether outside or inside, we were all just waiting for black smoke, hoping to get it over with so we could go get some dinner and then, hopefully, some sleep.

As smoke began to billow out of the chimney, I thought to myself, *Finally. We can go home for the night.* But then…white smoke. *White smoke?*

I was floored. I couldn't believe they'd made the decision by the fifth ballot. A pope this soon? What did it mean? *Who* did it mean?

Dolan was our man! I had goosebumps just thinking about the possibility that he might be the new pope. It made sense to me: The cardinals couldn't agree upon a European or (excuse me for being racist) black pope by the fourth ballot…on the fifth ballot, they went in a different direction: To the guy with evangelical swagger and universal charm. I could picture him dressed in white, laughing and joking as he smacked his brother cardinals on the back in his folksy, Midwestern style: "All right, way to go! Good voting, guys. Hot diggity, I'm the new pope!" I got emotional just thinking about it. And I couldn't stop thinking about it.

As a broadcaster, I kept that possibility, and others, alive. Perhaps Dolan. Perhaps Scola. Perhaps an African. And then I worried about accusations of reverse racism if they didn't pick a pope from Africa. You could hear the analysts say, "Wow, the Catholic Church is racist. Not a black pope."

An hour or so later, Cardinal Jean-Louis Tauran came out onto the balcony. Well, now that he was out there, I knew for sure one guy who didn't get elected: Him. That was one cardinal down, 114 to go.

After he announced, *"Habemus Papam!"* I recalled eight years earlier looking at that same balcony, wondering who the new pope would be. As Yogi Berra would say, "It was like déjà vu all over again."

For a moment, I thought of how hilarious it would be if the cardinals had elected Ratzinger again. The uncomfortable phone call: "Umm, yeah, hi, Pope Emeritus? Good news and bad news. Good news is we've elected a pope. Bad news is…well, we're sending the helicopter over to pick you up. We'll tell you more when we see you."

Seeing that as a faint possibility, I was prepared for whatever name Tauran would announce. And unlike in 2005, this time I'd practiced my Latin. I had memorized the first names of the front-runners in Latin: Angelum was Angelo; Marcum was Marc; Timotheum was Timothy.

Cardinal Tauran then gave us the news: *"Eminentissimum ac*

Reverendissimum Dominum, Dominum Georgium Marium."

Georgium Marium? Unlike when Josephum was announced and the crowds cheered, this time the throngs were mostly silent. I was stunned. And I was on the air. Who is George Mary?

"Sanctæ Romanæ Ecclesiæ Cardinalem Bergoglio," Tauran continued, *"qui sibi nomen imposuit Franciscum."*

Bergoglio? The guy I said had no chance to win? Great. Hope he didn't listen to the tapes. And he took the name Francis…one of the greatest saints in Church history. Can he do that?

For the next few minutes, as we waited the arrival of this new pope, I could only express my shock at the decision. And admit my embarrassment that two hours earlier I was on the air explaining why he wouldn't be elected. I also corrected my prediction from earlier in the broadcast when I declared that whoever the next pope was, he'd take the name Paul VII. I was on fire. I only wished I were in Vegas to keep that winning streak going.

When the curtains opened, and this man we knew almost nothing about stepped onto the balcony, it was bizarre. He just stared at the crowd. It was like a staring contest: Who would blink first? The pope or the crowds?

The cardinals had picked a seventy-six-year-old mute who stared at the world. He wasn't smiling. It was creepy. He put his hand up as if to wave, but there was almost no movement in his arm. Did they choose a mannequin? On air, I tried to spin it positively by saying, "He's probably stunned." In reality, I was thinking, *Yeah, this is going well.* I was afraid he was going to turn around and walk away. Two minutes passed. The microphone arrived. He prepared to speak.

And then he did. *"Fratelli e sorelle. Buona sera."* And he smiled.

Wait. He just said, "Brothers and Sisters. Good evening." I liked it. Very casual. That was different for a pope.

"You know that it was the duty of the conclave to give Rome a bishop. It seems that my brother cardinals have gone to the ends of the earth to get one."

He made a joke. He was getting laughs. And he was laughing. I liked him more.

"But here we are. I thank you for your welcome. The diocesan community of Rome now has its bishop. Thank you!"

He was talking like a Roman. Like an Italian. Interesting. And then, he asked for prayers for Bishop Emeritus Benedict XVI. He didn't say *pope*; he said, *bishop*. That was different. And then, talk about different, he led us in prayer with an Our Father, a Hail Mary, and a Glory Be.

Praying. Yeah, that makes perfect sense. In fact, I suddenly realized it was strange that previous popes hadn't done this.

"And now I would like to give the blessing, but first—first I ask a favor of you: Before the bishop blesses his people, I ask you to pray to the Lord that he will bless me: the prayer of the people asking the blessing for their bishop. Let us make, in silence, this prayer: your prayer over me."

I couldn't believe what I was hearing. Even with my rudimentary Italian, I understood he was bowing down to ask for prayers. But for tens of thousands of folks in the piazza who didn't speak Italian, they had no idea what was going on. For all they knew, they thought the new pope had stomach cramps and bent over, needing to take a breather.

Cardinal Dolan would tell me afterward that he and some of his brother cardinals were standing in the wings and—since there were no speakers near them—they couldn't hear what the pope said. So when Francis went quiet, and the crowds equally quiet, the cardinals had no idea what was going on. *Did he just abdicate? Are we voting again?*

Francis then gave us his apostolic blessing. Unlike with Benedict, I didn't kneel down. I was still on the air, after all. But I did, once again, feel blessed to have his first blessing.

The microphone was taken away but the pope was still there, taking in the cheers of the crowds chanting "*Viva il Papa!*" Waving. Smiling. And then he did something even stranger. He asked for the mic back. It was if he wanted to do an encore. He was just warming up!

"Brothers and sisters, I leave you now. Thank you for your welcome. Pray for me and until we meet again. We will see each other soon. Tomorrow I wish to go and pray to Our Lady, that she may watch over all of Rome. Good night and sleep well!"

Well, "Good night and sleep well" is the official Vatican translation. But what you might not get if you don't speak the language is how informally he was speaking. He was talking not like a pope but like a friend. *Buona notte e buon riposo* is something you'd say to someone you know well. *Good night, sleep tight.* Plus, I loved that he just casually mentioned we'll see each other soon and would be praying at a church tomorrow, just FYI.

"This might just be a pope who does his own thing," I said on the air that night. Boy, was I right. (For the first time.) "He seems very comfortable in his own skin."

Several hours later, I appeared on CNN's *Piers Morgan Live.* It was my third night in a row on the show, and I didn't hold my enthusiasm back. I declared with great joy that Francis is a man who says, "I'm going my own way."

We celebrated on air. We celebrated off air. After my work was done, I walked to St. Peter's Square to reflect on it all. The piazza was empty, of course. It was 3:00 A.M., and everyone was long gone. I stared at that empty balcony and thought about not just tonight, but all such nights the Church has had over the centuries. All the popes who have stood on that balcony in the four hundred years since it was built, let alone the almost two thousand years of popes we've had.

This is why the Church survives, I thought. *Because the Holy Spirit is filled with surprises.* It's our job to listen and follow. And in spite of the criticisms that I and many Catholics have had with Church leadership at times, this was a night when I realized that we got it right. From the drama and theater of white smoke…to the princes of the Church praying for our next pope. It works. Human and divine; sacred and profane. In one big pope-a-palooza.

The next morning, the first of his pontificate, he visited one of the major basilicas in the city: St. Mary Major. After praying in front of the icon of Our Lady, Patroness of Rome, he left some flowers on the altar.

As good fortune would have it, I was not only broadcasting from Rome, but also leading a group of listeners on pilgrimage that week. We happened to be scheduled to have Mass at that very church, on that very altar, on that same day. So, just hours after Pope Francis made his papal visit and left the papal flowers, I was at the same altar with my friend Fr. Jim Chern as he prepared to celebrate Mass there. People on our trip wanted to touch items to the flowers as if they were already second-class relics. Francis had been pope one day, certainly not canonized yet, but we wanted to touch the flowers he touched only hours beforehand because his holiness was that obvious. That's a saint.

I saw him in person several times during the first week of his papacy. And what I saw was a Christian. The guy is, just simply, Christian. He's humble. He cares for the poor. He loves everyone. The cardinals couldn't have picked a better guy. He excites us to live Christianity with joy, in service to others. A guy who, quite frankly, I knew nothing about. Who I thought could not possibly be what the Church needs. But a guy who inspires me to be a better Christian. That's the future.

CHAPTER TWENTY-ONE

THE SOUNDTRACK OF MY LIFE

WHEN I'M MADE A SAINT,
I hope to hold the record among the canonized for the number of air
miles logged. I'm nearly as obsessed with hitting the million-mile mark
as I am with becoming a saint. I love to travel, but, just as I don't look
forward to the dying part of sainthood, my least favorite part of a trip is
the leaving part. I'm always stressed out. I'm afraid I've packed poorly and
have forgotten something mildly important—and I always do. A camera,
deodorant, pants. Things you'd think I'd remember, considering how
much I've traveled.

Once I've zipped up my poorly packed bag and set it by my front door,
I begin my departure ritual. This begins with walking around my home
and saying final prayers. I start in the living room, where I touch a second-
class relic of John Paul II and ask for his intercession. I then head into my
bedroom, where I stand in front of a Franciscan cross, touching the feet
of Jesus and asking for His mercy. Next, I look around my apartment one
last time, wishing I wasn't leaving. Wishing, instead, that I could cancel
my plans at the last minute and just spend the night in my living room. I
look at the couch and bid it a fond farewell with as much tenderness as I
would have in saying good-bye to an old friend.

The next part of my departure ritual includes the realization that I'm
late for my flight. I grab my bag, run out of my apartment, get in the
elevator, hail a cab. That's when it hits me: I forgot to lock the door. I am

convinced. At the beginning of some trips, I'm not even sure I *closed* the door. I try to picture myself shutting it, the way the doorknob felt in my hand when I pulled it closed, the vision of my keys in the lock, but when I close my eyes, I can't see any of it. I fill this emptiness with visions of my door wide open, the entire holy contents of my apartment in peril. I could go back and check the door, but since I'm already running late, at this point in the ritual I just have to hope I didn't leave the door wide open.

Once I'm at the airport, I find that I can't eat. I'm too nervous to eat. In addition, while most people are afraid of getting food poisoning at their destination, I'm afraid of getting it before I arrive. If I do, it'll keep me up all night. If it's a long flight, I'll be stuck in the lavatory. Maybe the plane will crash when I'm in there. Maybe the NTSB, when they detail the events of my doomed flight, will note that the passenger in 2A—one *Leno* Rulli—was found not in his seat, but in the ruins of the first-class toilet. Maybe they'll note that when investigators went to his apartment to notify his family of his death, they found the door wide open and no one and nothing inside.

I'm not joking when I say that I really do think every flight might be my last. When I'm boarding, I look around at my fellow passengers and wonder if these are the people I'm destined to die with. *Does this look like the typical group of doomed folks I've seen in plane crash movies? Does that businessman have any clue what's about to happen? How about the lady holding the toddler? Doesn't she care about her kid? Or the couple who's taking a fiftieth-anniversary trip? Would they board if they knew their marriage and this plane were soon going to explode in an enormous fireball?*

And yet, despite these thoughts, I join them. I travel because I love it. And once I arrive at my destination, at some point on the trip—perhaps to replace these obsessively morbid thoughts with obsessively wistful ones—I take out my iPhone and listen to my favorite music. Before there was an iPhone, I took out my iPod; before that, a portable CD player with shoulder strap and headphones; and before that, I just hummed tunes in my head.

I started a playlist in 1995. It evolves. I add songs. I delete them. Each song means something to me in a way that—as is true with all art forms— the artist never imagined or intended. There are now twenty-nine songs, but I don't listen to all of them on every trip. Sometimes I'm not in the mood; sometimes I don't have the time. In fact, I'm not even listing them all here for the same reason I don't listen to them all: I'm not in the mood.

I've labeled it "Z Best," because, unlike so many things when I'm traveling, it's easy for me to find. I've listened to these songs while walking through Red Square in Moscow. Climbing Machu Picchu in Peru. Standing at the top of Mt. Sinai in Egypt. Walking the Great Wall of China in, well, China. On safari in South Africa. Roaming through the gardens of Tokyo. And every year for my birthday while standing in St. Peter's Square in Rome. Though it's labeled "Z Best," I think of it as The Soundtrack of My Life. That's right, you heard me: The Soundtrack of My Life. (I just vomited a little in my mouth after saying that out loud).

I dedicate this chapter to my friend Fr. Rob Keighron. Because nobody hates me talking about these things more than him. This one's for you, Fr. Rob.

"Hey There Delilah" by Plain White T's

I have no idea why this is on my playlist. Let alone why it's the first song on the list. It's got this melancholy guitar sound I like, a whiny guy singing that I like—and who doesn't like songs about women named Delilah? There's a line in the song that asks, "What's it like in New York City?" that really resonates with me as I live there. Wherever I'm standing on earth, I wonder what it's like back in NYC. My open-doored apartment, my friends, the urine-filled streets…

In my day-to-day life, I have a tendency to be completely absorbed with wherever I am. When I'm in NYC, I forget about Moscow. When I'm in Moscow, I forget about Venice. And so on. I have a very myopic view of the world and too easily forget about other places. This song helps remind me of my home in New York. And I guess about women named Delilah. I can say, without a shadow of a doubt, it's the greatest song ever dedicated to a girl named Delilah. Ever.

"Wish You Were Here" by Pink Floyd

This song is perfect because it can refer to anyone I "wished was here" at that particular moment: Mom, Pops, family members, friends, girl-friends...well, ex-girlfriends. I'm not wishing they are *all* with me at the same time. That sounds like a nightmare, actually. But different places make me wish certain folks were with me. Two specific girls who, if I hadn't been so stupid, egotistical, and selfish (in other words, what makes me *me*), might really be here. Who knows if they'd actually want to be with me in these crazy places, though? When I listen to this song, I think about whoever is on my mind at that particular point in time, people alive and dead.

"Yellow" by Coldplay

I know only two Coldplay songs. This is one of them. Oddly enough, I don't know if I even like this song. And other than Big Bird, I don't like the color yellow. I think my reasoning for liking the song is biblical. There's a line that points to the book of Genesis: "Look at the stars, look how they shine for you." So when I'm listening to this song, especially at night, I like to think that God created the heavens, the galaxies, and the stars just for me at that moment. To look at His creation and marvel at what He's given us. Well, given me.

"Boulevard of Broken Dreams" by Green Day

The song opens with a line about walking a "lonely road." I intentionally listen to this one while walking—down a boulevard, an alley, or a main street someplace on earth. The name of the song makes perfect sense to me. I can think of so many dreams I had that are now gone.

There was a time I dreamed of being a great media success. Gone.

A time I dreamed of being in great physical shape. Nope.

The time I dreamed my therapy would eventually make me less crazy. Hah.

I'm by myself, walking alone, but I know God is with me. So I'm not really alone. But I feel alone. But I'm not. But…

"Keep Me in Your Heart" by Warren Zevon

Because I'm such a Letterman fan, I'm influenced by him—and he likes this Zevon character. From what I understand he wrote it after being diagnosed with mesothelioma and knowing he was going to die. I guess it's a song asking, basically, to be remembered after he's gone. It's a terribly sad song, which is weird since I usually listen to it on vacation when I'm in great spirits. But it reminds me of my own mortality.

I particularly love listening to this song when looking at ancient brickwork or stone masonry. Stick with me here. Maybe it's the stones in the pyramids of Egypt; maybe it's the ruins of an ancient temple. I think about the day laborer who worked there. It was his craft. He put in his time, went home, maybe to a wife and kids. He had his life, he contributed, and he died. That's it. The world doesn't remember his name, but I can see his work.

Life will go on after I'm gone, too. And, just maybe, this points to why I want to be canonized: *to be remembered.* Don't we all want that, in some way? To have the world remember we were here, and to know we made some contribution? Well, I do. I'd like to be in your heart not just for a while, but for eternity.

"Home" by Foo Fighters
"Home Sweet Home" by Mötley Crüe
"Long Walk Home" by Bruce Springsteen

I play these songs back-to-back-to-back because they all have to do with the theme of home. And since I'm listening to them when I'm out of the country, it reminds me of, you guessed it, home. Not New York City, which is exclusively for Delilah, but *home* home: St. Paul, Minnesota. My family, my friends, the Christmas tree in our sitting room, my pets that have died, and everything that comes with the city. I know I've *chosen* to go to whatever country I'm in. But I always kinda wish I had stayed home. I wish I hadn't gotten on the plane.

"Lose Yourself" by Eminem

I added this to my playlist in 2003, during a particularly career-driven point in my life. I was so completely committed to my career and wanting to become a success that I felt I needed a song to motivate me. I wanted to win in my career the way Eminem wins a rap battle. As strange as it sounds, in retrospect, I was determined to make myself a success. *Feet don't fail me now!* At the end of the song, he says "You can do anything you set your mind to, man." I listen to those words now and laugh. I love Eminem, but that's not really true. I can't do anything I set my mind to. I can't become an astronaut or Miss America. But, with God's help, maybe I can do whatever He's got in His mind for my life.

"Cat's in the Cradle" by Harry Chapin

This is a song about fathers and sons, and in the song the son becomes just like his dad. I've got so many qualities from both my mom and dad, but I don't know any songs about moms and sons that are this reflective. The first time I realized how much I had become my dad was at the Acropolis, in Athens, Greece. When I was a kid, we'd go on a family vacation and

Pops would march us up and down every street, back alley, and crevice of every town. Our legs would be burning, and Mom and I just wanted a respite at the end of the night. When I was by myself, in Athens, I walked the entire day. Including up the hill to the Acropolis. I heard this song and realized I had become my dad. The good and the bad. And my legs hurt.

"What Difference Does It Make?" by The Smiths

I listened to this song incessantly in the tenth grade, the height of my the-devil-will-find-work-for-idle-hands-to-do years. And now, when I listen to this song, I think about all my travel. All my work. All the stress I'm trying to run away from on vacation. And, as the title asks, what difference does it make? Good question.

"Damn Good" by David Lee Roth

I'll be honest—this song isn't that great. But one night back in 1988, a bunch of high-school buddies and I were in our mall parking lot drinking beer, and this song was playing. I thought to myself, way back then, *Someday we'll be adults and look back on these days....* Yes, I was nostalgic for my youth even when I was still a youth.

"Behind Blue Eyes" by Limp Bizkit

This is a tough one to explain, since I don't actually have blue eyes. But no one knows what it's like to be in my shoes. (Not that I know what it's like to be in anyone else's shoes, because I'm a germaphobe, and the idea of sharing shoes is gross.)

"The Wrestler" by Bruce Springsteen

I love the movie. Mickey Rourke is awesome in it, and I was happy that this film gave him another chance at success. I'm a big fan of second chances. The opening line talks about being like a one-trick pony in the field, "happy and free." I feel so happy and free when I'm traveling. Look at what I'm listening to: The Soundtrack of My Life! No matter where I go, I listen to these songs. I reflect. This is how God made me. I think this song sums me up all too well. I'm a one-trick pony.

"Everlong" by Foo Fighters

This is my favorite song of all time. In fact, I try to be very cautious how often I hear the song. It opens simply: "Hello, I've waited here for you... everlong."

I'll sound like a mental patient right now, but in a sense I think these places—some of which have been there for thousands of years—have waited for me. And so, in the chorus, when Dave Grohl asks—"If everything could ever feel this real forever...if anything could ever be this good again..."—I ask myself the same question. *What will heaven be like? Will it be better than this?*

This is always the last song I listen to. I then turn the music off, take the earbuds out, and look around at the people who, undoubtedly, have had a laugh watching me rock out for the past half hour or so.

I know this might not seem like the playlist of a canonized saint. No Christian music here; nothing about praising God, no Requiem Mass. Yet, my playlist helps me reflect, as a saint should. As I listen, I think about where I've been in my life. My ego, my sins, my lust—they're pretty ingrained. I ask myself where I'm going. I know I don't deserve to be in heaven, and I know I can't earn it. I think of the many places I've listened to these songs, during times of worry, doubt, happiness, or peace. And, not knowing where I'll be next time I hear these songs again, I leave it in God's hands.

: SAINT :

CHAPTER TWENTY-TWO

ST. PAT DRIVES THE LADIES OUT OF THE HOT TUB

I'VE NEVER BEEN MARRIED. AND I've been single for most of my adult life. Some think it's because I work too much. Others think it's because I'm too picky. Women say it's because I'm ugly. I think I'm alone because I have a friend named Pat. Ever since I met him in my sophomore year of college, he has ruined more relationships for me than my personality, social awkwardness, and fear of commitment combined.

In the Our Father, we pray, "Forgive us our trespasses as we forgive those who trespass against us." Since I go to confession frequently, you'd think I'd be pretty good at forgiving people as often as God forgives me. And you'd be wrong. When it comes to Pat, however, I've had a lot of opportunities to flex my forgiveness muscles and grow like a bodybuilder in holiness. When Peter asked Jesus how many times he should forgive someone, the Lord said, "Seventy times seven." According to my math, that's 490 reps of forgiveness. With Pat, I've almost reached my workout goal.

It's 1991. I'm sporting a mullet, a flannel shirt, and my Girbaud jeans are rolled up at the bottom. We're at a bar. C&C Music Factory's less popular hits are playing in the background. I'm talking to a girl with huge hair, wearing a pound and a half of makeup, and a sweatshirt conspicuously wrapped around her waist. I presume she has a big butt, and that's her way of hiding it. I only wish I could wrap a sweatshirt around my face to hide that from the world.

Needless to say, I'm not in a picky mood. We're talking music, and I give her my take on why the band Extreme is not a one-hit wonder and why their one-hit thus far, "More Than Words," will surely be around for decades. I think I'm making progress. I'm about to get a number. Maybe seven numbers. But then Pat walks up.

"Oh, is this the girl you've been telling me all about?" he asks me. And then he turns to her. "It's so great to meet you in person. Lino talks about you all the time."

Of course, because I just met her, she immediately feels like he's confused her for someone else—someone I'm really interested in and talk about all the time. Before I can correct the situation, she's moved on. I spot her by the bar, listening to some other guy's take on early 90s music. This guy doesn't have a friend like Pat. But I do, and I'm stuck drinking with him for another evening.

Forgiveness.

The summer of 1997, I was twenty-seven years old and living in Minneapolis with two roommates: the aforementioned Pat, and Dan—a friend of ours from college. All three of us were unemployed, living in what is known as a starter home. Not as in *start to grow up*. Not as in *start to look for a job*. As in *start to drink before lunch*.

The living room had a beautiful picture window that allowed the neighbors and passersby a clear view of us lounging on their way to work. Unfortunately, we couldn't afford air conditioning. Which was fine, because the house didn't have an air conditioning system. So every day the three of us would sit, and sweat, and stick to the leather couch as we flipped between *The Price is Right* and MTV. Since the picture window didn't open, our only chance for fresh air was to keep the front door open and hope a breeze would pass through the screen.

Every day, the mailman delivered magazines in black wrappers and bills we couldn't pay. "Hey guys," he'd say.

"Hey, Joe."

No doubt, Joe was a bit "jealgry"—what we said when someone was jealous of and angry at us at the same time. Jealous that he couldn't sit around with *his* friends, drinking beer while sitting on the couch. Angry that otherwise able-bodied guys were living their lives in such a carefree way.

At some point, one of us would ask, "What are we going to do today?"

The biggest tasks—chores like buying stamps and mailing letters—had to wait until the end of the day when the temperatures dropped.

As summer came to a close, Dan disappointed us by moving on to, as he put it, "grow up and get married."

Pat and I grew up a bit. We found almost full-time work, which meant we were able to scrape together enough money to do what we really wanted to do with our lives, as well: Get a hot tub. Unlike Dan, instead of settling down with a wife, we chose a hundred-dollar-a-month hot tub as our partner in this next stage of our lives.

The hot tub was delivered on a beautiful fall day. Our neighbors were a couple in their early sixties, eternally patient with the twentysomething losers next door. The husband, Oliver, stopped by to see what we were up to. "Hot tub, huh? You rent it for the weekend?" At the time, we thought he was jealgry, but, looking back, he was probably wondering how long he'd have to endure the noise of late-night hot tub parties.

"Nope," we told him. "We've rented it for six months." The sadness in the air was palpable.

Not for us, though. Pat and I got busy jamming the six-person hot tub into the one-car garage, pushing aside the lawnmower, shovels, and dead bodies to make room for it.

"It's as if the garage was *made* for this hot tub," Pat said.

Except for the lack of an outlet, he was right. To power the hot tub and a thirteen-inch TV that we propped up on a tool chest next to the tub, we ran an extension cord a mere twenty-five yards from the garage to the house. Sure, we'd have to keep my bedroom window open a couple inches, exposed to the temperatures and snowdrifts of a typical Minnesota winter, but that tiny sacrifice would be worth it. After all, whenever I was cold in my bedroom I could always run outside and take a nice warm soak.

Our first few weekends with the tub went pretty much as expected: We'd go to a bar, bump into old friends from high school or college, and end up having people come back for a soak in the tub. I think most folks came over just to see if we really were fully functioning adult males with a fully functioning hot tub in our garage. The answer was yes. Sometimes it was guy friends; sometimes it was female friends. Occasionally I'd be creepy enough to meet a girl at the bar and ask if she'd like to come check out our tub. She'd say no. The end. Pat had a girlfriend at the time, so "the end" for him wasn't as final as it was for me.

One Saturday, however, my luck changed. Two sisters we'd recently become friends with heard the neighborhood buzz about the hot tub. They called to ask if they could come over and see it. I checked the calendar. Umm, yes, we were available to show them the hot tub. I penciled them in. That night, before they arrived, we went out to a bar where the unthinkable happened: I met a girl who said yes. Her name was Nicole, and she and I really hit it off. She decided that she—and her friends—wanted to come over to see the tub. We left the bar; they stopped home to get some swimsuits and showed up ready to get in.

It was midnight, there were five girls in bikinis, and I was the only single guy in sight. And my buddy Pat, serving as my wingman. What could go wrong?

As President George W. Bush once so eloquently said, "Fool me once, shame on...shame on you. Fool me, we can't get fooled again." In my case, well, yes, I'd get fooled again. Shame on me.

Before getting into the hot tub—that is, before Nicole saw me without a shirt—I asked if I could take her out sometime.

"Of course we're going to go out, silly. Did you think I came over here for a hot tub in a garage?"

Good point. "Can I get your number?" I asked.

"When we get out of the tub," she promised.

While I was busy laying the groundwork with one of Nicole's friends— hoping to establish that I was a really nice guy who, though he had a hot tub in a garage, had nothing but good intentions and a stunning career ahead of him—Pat was busy talking to Nicole.

It's hard to hold a conversation with one girl in a hot tub while trying to listen to the conversation of another, especially when there are three other voices and a thirteen-inch TV adding to the cacophony.

"But what you're saying is really offensive." Uh-oh. Was that Nicole?

"Well, I just think a woman's place is in the kitchen, that's all." That was definitely Pat. "What, just because I'm a ditch digger, I can't have an opinion?" That was Pat, too. Even though he wasn't a ditch digger, I recognized his voice.

"Honestly, it has nothing to do with your job." Good, Nicole sounded like she was calming down.

Maybe I could get in front of this accident waiting to happen and, well, keep it from happening. I couldn't maneuver fast enough around the tubful of girls.

"It's just…I can't have a conversation like this. I think it's time to go home." Nicole was getting out of the hot tub. I followed her.

I caught up with her outside the garage, as she was gathering her things. "Hey, sorry about my friend," I said. "He was just joking around."

"Well, if that was a joke, he sure has a weird sense of humor."

I could hear her friends getting out of the tub. It wouldn't be long before they'd be surrounding her with good judgment.

"I agree. Weird sense of humor. Very weird. Right. But anyway, we're still going out, right? Can I get your phone number?"

"Sorry," she said. "Guilt by association."

She got her things and headed for her car, leaving me with mixed emotions. She looked amazing. But unfortunately, she looked amazing as she was *walking away from me.*

At least there were two other girls I might have a chance with, right? By time I returned to the hot tub, I heard one of them say to Pat, "I can't believe you just said that about my grandmother!"

Hmm. Insulting a person's grandmother is typically not a sign of good things to come. Thus, the sisters left, as well.

Forgiveness.

In 2000, my luck with dating changed slightly. Not because I got better looking or changed my style—or my take on 90s music—but because I was on television. I was hosting a TV show at the time, and for reasons I have yet to understand, nor have even examined very much, women like a guy on TV. It doesn't matter if you're a local reporter, a cable-access host, or being interviewed after your house burned down. You're on TV? You've got a shot with the ladies.

Unless Pat's around to shoot any chances down before they take flight.

One cold Minnesota winter's night, the two of us were over-served at a local bar. That's the only explanation I have as to how we got so drunk. As we literally stumbled out of the establishment, a girl was at the doorway just coming in.

"Lino!" she yelled.

"Me!" I yelled back at her.

"I think you're so funny. I love your TV show."

This was my type of girl. Because of the booze, she was several of my types of girl, but I tried concentrating on the middle version of her. Unfortunately, I was too drunk to make a coherent sentence and instead had to make a confession: "I'm sorry. I'd love to talk to you, but I'm too drunk right now." And with that, I headed home.

Nearly a year later, Pat and I were at a bar again, and who do I see walking up to me but the girl I recognized as the one in the middle! This time, thankfully, I only had a few drinks in me, and I was able to have an actual human conversation.

We hit it off, I asked for her number, and she gave me her business card. It struck me as a cold gesture. The card had just her work number and e-mail address, but then again, the last time she saw me I was one drink away from pulling a Hasselhoff and eating off the floor. Not exactly the kind of guy a girl would want phoning at one in the morning.

Business card in hand, I went off to talk to some other friends at the bar. As if we were back in the hot tub, I noticed Pat was talking to her, as well. I started to regret introducing them.

Later, he found me. "That's weird, that girl you were talking to gave me her phone number."

"What? Why would she do that? You have a girlfriend. Why would she give you her number?"

"I don't know. I didn't ask for it. She just offered it to me."

I made him show it to me. He took out a piece of paper from his pocket. And there, in the middle of a bunch of notes, was a phone number. I'd gotten a business card, but she'd given Pat a home phone number written in her own lovely hand? I lost it. She had made me look like an idiot. I thought she liked me. Turns out, she was the kind of girl who gave her number to everyone she met. I stormed up to where she was sitting at the bar.

"Do you think I'm a moron?"

She took a moment to consider her answer. "What are you talking about?"

"That guy you gave your phone number to? That's my roommate. You didn't think I was going to find out? Oh, by the way, he's got a girlfriend so he won't be calling you anyway."

Surprisingly she wasn't angry or defensive. She was patient. "Lino, I have no idea what you are talking about."

"Whatever. I'm not stupid. And this time I'm not drunk. You gave me your number. You gave my roommate your number. Who knows who else you'll give your number to."

I might as well have called her a phone number tramp. She was very loose when it came to giving out those digits.

"I'm outta here," I said. I looked to my friend Pat—my good friend Pat who's always looking out for me—and said, "Let's go. We don't need people like this in our lives."

And with that declarative statement on her humanity and morals, or lack thereof, we left the bar. Outside, Pat and I got in a cab and headed home.

"You know, it really bugs me," I said. "I liked that girl. I see her after more than a year of thinking about her, and it turns out she was more interested in you than in me."

Pat laughed.

"What?" I asked.

"I made it up," he said.

"Huh?"

"I didn't really get her phone number."

"The paper," I said. "I saw it on the paper."

He took it out of his pocket again. "That's the number of a guy I work with. I wrote it down a few months ago. Don't know why I haven't thrown it away." He shoved it back in his pocket, a crumpled up memory of a joke on me.

To this day I'm sure that girl has no idea why I flipped out and yelled at her. To her, I offer my apologies. Forgive me my verbal trespasses, as I've forgiven Pat who has seriously and repeatedly trespassed against me.

It's easy for someone unfamiliar with our brand of friendship to ask why I'm still friends with Pat after all these years.

Perhaps it's because I don't make friends easily. But I also think it's because of gags like this that we're still actually friends. The sign of a good friendship is how poorly you treat each other and yet still remain friends.

My friends strengthen my case for canonization. They aren't all holy, pious, perfect folks. They don't always treat me well. They might even be considered drunkards and gluttons. I can think of someone else who had friends like that: Jesus Christ. He was accused of hanging out with gluttons, drunkards, and prostitutes. I can say that my friends fit only in the first two categories—to the best of my knowledge, anyway.

And as anyone will tell you, perhaps Jesus included, these types of folks are more fun to hang out with. The Lord came to rescue the lost sheep, to minister to the sick. But let's face it, even He didn't want to have dinner with the Pharisees and Sadducees every night. Pious, self-righteous folks just don't make good dinner company. Jesus knew that.

I figure Jesus didn't pick the best of friends, and it turned out OK. Peter denied Him three times. Judas sold the Lord out for thirty pieces of silver. At the crucifixion, everyone but John ran away. And those were the twelve apostles! Jesus and the twelve, like most friends, probably had inside jokes. Stories shared. Bonds built.

Though I'm not one of his original twelve, I try to treat my relationship with Jesus as a friendship. When things aren't going my way, when I feel Jesus isn't treating me like a friend, I talk to Him just the way I'd talk to Pat, or any other friend.

There's that miserable train wreck of a song, "What a Friend We Have in Jesus." Whoever wrote that song must not have had any friends, because their friends would have said, "Hey, that song really sucks." That's what friends are really for.

Nevertheless, the words are true. My prayers to my friend Jesus aren't always as holy and reverent as perhaps they should be. But I figure He wants honesty. And He's God—He knows what I'm really thinking anyway. So if I pray, "O loving and good God, I thank Thee for this blessed day" when I'm really thinking, "O God, today sucked," I'm only kidding myself.

My friendship with Pat reminds me of a story about Teresa of Avila. When things weren't going her way, she complained to the Lord, and Jesus said, "This is how I treat my friends." To which the great saint replied, "No wonder you have so few of them."

I'm a saint, see? I've dealt with Pat's antics for more than twenty years and I still consider him my friend. No wonder I have so few of them. Look how they treat me.

: CHAPTER TWENTY-THREE :

OH MERCY, MERCY ME

AT THIS POINT IN THE
book you may be thinking to yourself: *Hey, if Lino is able to become a
saint...I could be one, too!*

Well, welcome to the club. Use this form to see if you are a candidate to
become a canonized saint in the Catholic Church.

Please check these boxes to see if you're on your way to canonization:

☐ You are Catholic.

☐ You are real (sorry St. Christopher).

☐ You are dead.

If you checked all three, please contact the Vatican and they will begin
processing your paperwork. Congrats!

By the way, there's no actual checklist before a person is canonized. The
Church, however, does offer us something called the "corporal works of
mercy," which are based on Jesus' words in Matthew 25:34–36.

> Come, O blessed of my Father, inherit the kingdom prepared
> for you from the foundation of the world; for I was hungry and
> you gave me food, I was thirsty and you gave me drink, I was
> a stranger and you welcomed me, I was naked and you clothed
> me, I was sick and you visited me, I was in prison and you came
> to me.

This is the basis for the corporal works of mercy, which I'll break down here to see how I've done.

☐ Feed the hungry

A few years ago I decided to go to a soup kitchen once a month and serve food to the hungry. Though it appeared to some that I was doing mandated community service, I swear it was voluntary.

I'd never volunteered in a soup kitchen before, primarily because I figured hungry people are tired of soup. They're hungry, sure, but they'd like a little variety, right? I was hoping to volunteer at a steak kitchen or a chicken teriyaki kitchen, but I never found one. Only soup kitchens.

I convinced three of my female friends to help me out. The four of us would go to the grocery store to pick up ingredients for whatever they wanted to cook. Since I don't know how to cook, my role was to help pay for the groceries. We then went to one of the girls' homes, where they made homemade lasagna, salad, and garlic bread. I was able to at least butter the garlic bread, so I wasn't completely useless.

It was a good feeling to go to a local men's homeless shelter with a home-cooked meal. We talked to the guys, told jokes, served them a second helping if they were real nice, and I looked forward to making this a part of my life.

OK, well, I planned on doing this every month. In reality, I only did it this one time. Somehow, life got in the way. Since then, I've taken the easy way out and just given my money to places that feed the hungry.

For Lent this past year, I decided to do some good old-fashioned alms-giving. When I didn't have any alms, I gave money instead. Every day, I gave at least ten dollars to folks who might need it. And living in New York, there are plenty who need help.

One night on my way home from work, I saw a guy asking for change. I knew I had a twenty-dollar bill in my pocket, but I also knew I wanted to buy dinner for myself. *Any chance*, I wondered, *he's got a ten-dollar bill on him?*

He caught me staring at him. "Hey buddy, you have any change?" he asked.

"Strangely enough," I said, "I was gonna ask you the same question. I've got a twenty-dollar bill here, and if you have a ten-dollar bill, I'd be happy to give you ten bucks."

He thought about what kind of scam I might be pulling. Maybe he was worried that I would give him a counterfeit bill? Or, if he had ten bucks, was I going to try to steal it from him? "No, I don't have a ten. Sorry."

"Tell you what," I replied, "I'm going to buy dinner and it costs about ten bucks. Come with me and you can spend the other ten."

We went to one of those classic New York delis that offer everything under the sun: pizza, burgers, sushi, salads, bagels, and every dessert possible. All without prices on them. You'd find out at the cash register. So I decided to make a little game of it.

"Now remember, I've only got twenty bucks. So we can spend every cent of it—but any more, and it comes out of your pocket."

He laughed. Then realized I was serious. Which made him laugh even more. It was like a game you'd see on *The Price Is Right*. "Guess the exact price of your item without going over, and you win!"

"I want a burger and fries," he said, "but will I have enough to get a drink?"

"Only one way to find out, my friend!" Being horrible at math, I had no idea. Turns out he had enough for a Snapple, but not for a beer.

When I told this story on the air, some listeners thought I was being mean-spirited or taunting him by allowing him to spend only ten bucks. But neither of us saw it that way at all. Often when I see people "less fortunate" than me, I don't treat them as normal—I treat them as different. In this case, though, I figured I could get him some food, and both of us could have some laughs along the way. Saints don't have to go around with a sourpuss expression on their face just because they're doing the right thing.

I say check this one off the list.

☐ Give drink to the thirsty

I've bought more than my share of rounds at a bar. Any chance that counts? Those folks needed drinks. If they were attractive women, all the better! Jesus wasn't specific about gender or dating status when it came to thirst. Thirst is thirst, my friends.

Certainly, if someone said, "These pretzels are making me thirsty!" I'd be happy to help with a beverage if I could. But the way Scripture describes giving drink to the thirsty seems much more like something from Jesus' day, like a guy walking through the desert, and you are near a well and are able to get him a drink.

Maybe I'm wrong on this one, but I think it's very limited. I have a feeling very few Christians are giving drink to the thirsty. Maybe standing on a street corner with bottles of water on a hot summer day is something I could do in the future.

If we're speaking literally, don't give me a check mark.

☐ Clothe the naked

Now to be fair, how often do I see naked people walking around? And if I go to a gentlemen's club and try to put clothes on the woman, I'll be promptly escorted away.

I do donate clothes to charity, but I have to admit it's more of a spring-cleaning process than a work of mercy. I've got shirts and pants hanging in the closet that I'm tired of wearing, and when I give those away I feel a little better about myself.

The old T-shirts and gym shorts that I give away could, technically, help clothe naked people. But you just don't see as many naked folks as you used to. Sign of the times, I guess.

The closest thing to sainthood I've done in this regard was to give away a pair of gloves. I thought this was a somewhat virtuous thing because when I had been in Iceland I'd bought a super-warm pair of gloves. (Mittens, actually. But *mittens* isn't the most masculine of words, which is why I'm calling them gloves for the sake of this story.)

One cold, blustery January day, I was driving home from work, and while I was stopped at a red light I saw a homeless guy sitting next to a building. Even though I was driving an old Jeep Wrangler that didn't have the greatest heating system, and I really liked my gloves, I knew that here was a guy who could use them even more.

I wasn't sure how to ask if he wanted them, because for all I knew he wasn't homeless at all. Maybe he just left work, forgot his gloves at the office, and was waiting for his limo driver to pick him up. Sure, he wasn't dressed all that well, but people could say the same thing about me on occasion. Nonetheless, I rolled my window down. "Hey buddy, are you cold?"

I immediately regretted that sentence. Being dumb has its consequences. Thankfully, he had a sense of humor. "Yeah, just a little!"

"Can I give you my gloves?" I asked. "I swear they're really warm. I got them in Iceland." Why I had to sell him on the Iceland element of the gloves, I have no idea.

"Sure," he said.

Putting the hazard lights on, I jumped out of the car and ran over to him. "There you go," I said, handing him my Icelandic-tested handwear.

He put them on, and agreed. "You're right, they're warm."

"God bless," I said. And I drove away.

So while I've never clothed a fully naked person, I've given some clothes away—and the mittens—so let's call it a tie. In fact, if it'll break the tie, I'll give a tie to a naked guy next time I see one.

☐ **Shelter the homeless**

I'm a little vague on how literally we're meant to take Jesus on this one. Does this mean I'm supposed to invite every person I see on the street into my home and say, "Come on in, you can have my bed! The combination to the safe is 10-26-71, by the way."

No, I don't think so. I mean, what pope invites random folks to crash at the Vatican for the night? Well, maybe Francis will. But he hasn't yet! So far, no popes have had homeless people sleep in their bed, and plenty of popes have become saints, so I must get a pass on that.

When I was a television reporter, I did a story about a homeless shelter and the wonderful Catholic woman who founded it. She took folks in, washed their feet, fed them, and gave them a place to sleep; it was truly inspiring.

But you haven't known awkward until you've interviewed a homeless person. First, you have to do a little profiling for the piece. You don't want to interview someone who looks too clean, or it won't help raise money from the viewers at home who might be open to giving. I know if I see a guy at the shelter dressed better than me, that's a deal breaker. At the same time, the person who looks distraught and mentally disturbed doesn't make for good television—except reality TV, of course.

I talked it over with my camera guy, and we came up with a few folks we thought fit our profiles.

"Excuse me, ma'am?" I said to a woman who seemed to be homeless (but not too homeless). "Can I ask you a few questions?"

She smiled. "Certainly."

And then came the personal questions that the viewer will never hear, but are so challenging to ask another human being who you've just met.

"How long have you been homeless?"

"Do you have any friends or family you can stay with?"

"What does having a place like this to visit mean to you?"

These questions might seem innocuous enough, but they're heartbreaking when a person has to answer them. Especially considering it's all just for television. I wasn't spending time with her to get to know her. I was getting a sound byte and trying to make sure that, if she teared up, my camera guy had the right angle.

And while I've never invited anyone into my home permanently, I do give money to homeless shelters. Only God will decide if that's enough.

No, I've never invited random people to crash on my couch, so I guess I can't check this one off the list.

☐ Visit the sick

Being a germaphobe, you can imagine how much I love this one. If I want to avoid germs, it stands to reason I definitely want to avoid sick people.

I once had a long-distance relationship with a girl I truly loved, and she came out for a visit to New York for a three-day weekend. Unfortunately, on the second day of her visit, she came down with a cold. And she was staying in my apartment! So even though I was sleeping on the couch, and she was sleeping upstairs in my bed, it was still *my* bed. And *my* stuff. Let's say it wasn't the most romantic two days, what with me refusing to hold hands or kiss her or touch anything she touched. And that was her visiting *me*. Jesus didn't say we'd get any points for the sick visiting us. He said we had to visit the sick.

I'm one of those folks who can't stand going to hospitals. The few times my loved ones have been in the hospital, I've tried to spend as little time there as possible. Germs aside, I'm just not the guy you want in those situations. I'm making jokes or saying stupid things. I don't have a consoling bone in my body and I'm never sure what to say.

"Hey, how's that leprosy going?" or, "On the plus side, I guess you'll lose weight after they remove that giant tumor!"

I do slightly better at nursing homes than I do hospitals, but not by much.

My grandfather Armando suffered from Alzheimer's and after my grandmother died, he was placed in a nursing home. The home itself was great—wonderful workers, beautiful environment—and I would visit him on occasion. Here was my big chance to visit the sick and check this off the list!

"Hey," he'd say when I walked in the room. You could tell he recognized my face; he just didn't know from where. Each time he'd have a new guess.

"Did we used to work together?" or, "You used to live down the block, right?" or, "You're the guy who owes me twenty bucks, aren't ya?"

"No, Grandpa," I'd say, "It's Lino. Angelo's son." I felt bad saying it, and the look in his eye gave me the sense he felt bad he didn't know me. What made the situation worse was that he recognized pretty much everyone else in the family.

He didn't know exactly where he was, in terms of a nursing home. He couldn't tell you the time and date, but he knew everyone. Everyone but me, that is.

As much as I hate to admit it, I couldn't stand the fact that he knew other people but not me. Whenever I stopped by, it was painful for both of us. I'm embarrassed to say it, but my visits became more and more infrequent.

When he passed away, I felt badly I hadn't visited him more often.

Fail. No checkmark. And I still wish I had been more virtuous and visited him more often, whether he knew me or not.

☐ Bury the dead

That's illegal. I'm Italian, and I know. I'm not falling for that one. Only licensed cemetery employees should be burying dead people.

Never buried a guy. No check and proud of it.

☐ Visiting the imprisoned

I've intentionally saved the best for last because I hope you'll only remember my virtue in this one area.

I used to do ministry at a maximum-security prison.

After a lengthy background check—presumably, the authorities wanted to see if, in fact, I had ever done the previous corporal work of mercy and buried a body, which, I repeat, I have not—I was allowed to do ministry.

A group of six of us (myself, two other guys, and three women) arrived for our first Monday night session. After checking in and going through several rounds of pat-downs, metal detectors, and general groping, we entered the prison.

Walking by the prisoners in their cells made me wonder: *Why didn't I sign up at a women's prison? That would have been the perfect fit for me. Even I would look like a real catch to those women. To someone who's incarcerated, I can be quite handsome.* But it was too late. I was at a man prison. And it was raining men.

The prison had a chapel and gathering space, which looked surprisingly like the inside of a typical suburban parish church. The six of us waited in the gathering space for the rest of the congregation to arrive, fifty or so parishioner-prisoners, who were led into the room by security and a chaplain.

The chaplain invited us all to get to know one another. Not surprisingly, the majority of the guys got in line to start chatting with the ladies.

Some of the others, either wanting to play it cool and let the girls come to them, or the guys who had already chatted with the women and realized there wasn't a spark, introduced themselves to us.

"Hey, how are you?" I said, while shaking the guy's hand, wondering what crimes might have been committed with those hands.

"Well, other than never being able to leave this place," he said, "everything is fine. How are you?"

I could tell I was going to like it here.

"What's new?" I continued on.

"Last night a guy put a shiv in my neck over a pack of cigarettes. You?"

I'm horrible at small talk as it is, but take away things like the weather (since he'd only be able to go outside an hour a day, so maybe that's mean), and I realized we better get talking about God.

Thankfully, the chaplain was a step ahead of us and invited us all to head into the chapel to begin Mass.

There were guys there who were murderers; they would never leave prison. And yet I could see that, in their hearts, they weren't in church out of some weird definition of obligation or to be entertained by a homily. That was some real heavy-duty praying going on in there.

There but for the grace of God go I, I thought. *I've made mistakes. I could have gone down some of the roads these guys did. But you saved me, Lord. Give me the faith these guys have.*

The Sign of Peace was, understandably, time-consuming, as the line formed behind the women once again.

After Mass ended, saying good-bye was always a delicate balance. Even though I'd see them the following week, I didn't want to rub it in. Like, "Hey, I'll be going outside to, well, do whatever I want as a free person. See you later!"

But this is a corporal work of mercy I can say I have, in fact, done. And would like to do again. Check!

OK, so let's add it up: 2–4–1? Well, that might hurt my chances for canonization. But hopefully I get brownie points for my honesty.

Run down the list for yourself and see if you do better than me. And hey, if you do, I'd be happy to suggest you for canonization, as well.

CHAPTER TWENTY-FOUR

ABOON DABASHMAYA

THOUGH BOTH OF MY PARENTS are Italian American, we didn't speak to each other in Italian at home. In fact, there were days we didn't speak to each other at all at home. That's another story.

In 1997, I moved to Italy to learn the language. Though my mother was a high-school French teacher for thirty years, I hadn't inherited her gift for foreign languages. After months of study I was only able to speak at a third-grade level. Thus, while I looked like every other guido, I had the distinct disadvantage of speaking like someone who'd had something very heavy dropped on his head. "My name is Lino. I like food. What are you called? Do you like food?"

Nonetheless, come Christmas of that year, like every other shmuck who spends a little time overseas, I sought to impress my friends, neighbors, and parole officer with the international flair that comes from speaking in a foreign tongue. And though I was far from fluent, I thought I could persuade people otherwise. Writing in Italian was the surefire way to do so.

I bought a stack of Christmas cards that featured an icon of the Virgin Mary and the Baby Jesus. "*Buon Natale,*" I wrote inside and "*Buon Anno Nuovo!*" Nothing fancy, just "Merry Christmas" and "Happy New Year!"

Yet, as I tackled the cards, something didn't look quite right. After much deliberation, I decided I had spelled the word *Anno* wrong and went with *Ano* instead, as in "*Buon Natale & Buon Ano Nuovo!*"

Being the perfectionist that I am, and wanting to make sure I was right, I consulted no one and put the cards in the mail.

Dropping an *n* when it comes to *funny* or *penny* is an obvious mistake. The writer has been careless, but the reader still gets the message. Unfortunately, dropping an *n* from *anno* changes the word altogether.

Anno means year. *Ano* means anus. And so, in the Year of our Lord, 1997, I wished my loved ones a Merry Christmas and a Happy New Anus.

Anuses aside (and when was the last time you saw that phrase in a Catholic book?), the positive aspect of struggling to learn Italian was that it brought me closer to God. That's because it was in Italy that I began to go to church regularly, which meant regularly worshipping in an unfamiliar language. Praying in Italian made me think of the Almighty in a new way. *God* was now *Dio*. *The Church* was *La Chiesa*. *Transubstantiation* was…well, I hadn't gotten that far.

At Mass, I prayed communally in Italian, which gave me the courage to pray privately in Italian, as well. Having a limited vocabulary in this new language made my prayers childlike. There's very little room for theological discourse and nuance when you don't know the future subjunctive tense of a verb. "God, let your will be done in all things and in all aspects of this ever-changing world" becomes "God, help me. Jesus, I love you."

These were the simple prayers of a future saint, for as Jesus pointed out in Matthew 18:3, "Truly, I say to you, unless you turn and become like children, you will never enter the kingdom of heaven."

This simplicity made the task of listening to God even more of a challenge. As Christians, we believe God does speak to us—not usually in an audible voice but in the silence of our hearts. Which caused my paranoia to kick in. Wouldn't it be my luck that the one time in my life that God would actually speak to me, He would do so in Italian, messing with me because He would know that I wasn't further along in my language studies?

Worshipping in another language stretched my mind even further when I joined the hundreds of thousands of people from around the world in St. Peter's Square and saw the universal Church in action: God hearing the prayers of South Americans, Filipinos, and Germans, all speaking in their own languages. The fact that He was hearing all their prayers helped me see God as conversant in every language.

I found myself realizing something fundamental about Jesus of Nazareth, something obvious that I should have considered long before: He didn't speak English. Sure, I pray to Him in English, but that wasn't His first tongue. In fact, if I were to pray the Our Father the way Jesus taught His apostles to pray, it would go something like this: "*Aboon dabashmaya nethkadash shamak tetha malkoothak…*"

Looks like a bunch of gibberish to me. And my spellcheck hates it. But that's Aramaic.

Jesus didn't use *thys* or *thines* when He prayed. I don't know why we still do, but I don't get to make those types of decisions. Yet. After being canonized, however, I'll put in a request that we make the Our Father more conversational. But we still have to wait for that…

One of the mysteries of Christianity is that it's so personal and yet so communal. Jesus is mine, but He's also yours. In fact, He's ours. God is ours. The saints are ours.

This notion that the saints are *ours* occurs to me at strange moments. I'll be praying in front of a statue of the Virgin Mary and someone will come up and kneel next to me. I want to say, "Hey, I'm praying here. Wait your turn." I'm afraid Mary's attention will transfer from me to the person next to me, and next thing you know I'm talking just to myself. This difficulty

I have in understanding how Mary could hear more than one prayer at a time is one reason I am devoted to lesser-known saints. St. Moses the Black and St. Gerlac of Valkenburg have very few people calling for their intercessions. They're all ears and more than happy to help out. They're just glad anyone remembers them.

When it comes to Mary, though, there are millions of people, all around the world, asking for her prayers in hundreds of languages. I can ask for her intercession and she hears my prayers though she never spoke English. The woman next to me can pray in French, and Mary hears her prayers. The kid next to me can offer his prayers in Kazakh (or whatever language he and Borat speak in Kazakhstan) and Mary hears his prayers, too.

I'm sure there's some boring theologian who can explain how the saints hear our prayers—and, coincidentally, that same theologian can simultaneously put everyone to sleep with the explanation—but I don't really care how it works. I just know *that* it works. The saints are outside of time and space; they're outside the limitations of language; and they hear our prayers. That's pretty heavy theology. It's getting into the whole "God's ways are above our ways" business about faith, which I find both fascinating and scary at the same time. I'm never really going to wrap my mind around the things of heaven this side of heaven, and I'm strangely OK with the uncertainty.

* * *

Though Italian brought me closer to God, other languages have not—primarily because when I try to take on a new language, it usually backfires. Case in point: The first time I went to Egypt, wanting to fit in, I decided to learn to speak a bit of Arabic beforehand. I bought a CD of "Easy-to-Learn" Arabic phrases.

Going into a predominantly Muslim country, I thought it'd be helpful to be able to say things like: "I'm Canadian"; "Which way is Mecca?"; and "Please don't cut my head off." After spending a few weeks learning the language as best I could, I was off—hopefully not head first.

A metal detector was waiting to greet me at my hotel in Cairo. A rather lethargic-looking guard presided over it, presumably there to prevent suicide bombers and attackers of all variety. It seems to me that hotels in the Middle East could take a lesson from construction sites in the US that have signs which proudly state "No Injuries for ___ Consecutive Days." I think it would be helpful to have something similar posted at the entrance to hotels. "No Suicide Bombers for ___ Consecutive Days" would be a solid signal as to what I'm getting myself into.

I walked through the metal detector, it beeped loudly, the guard stared at me blankly and waved me through. I was feeling more secure by the minute. I continued to the front desk ready to shine with my newly learned Arabic.

"*Sabah-hil hair,*" I said in Arabic. "*Kaef il hal, sayeed?*" I was pretty sure I'd just called him sir and asked him how he was doing.

"Sorry?" The hotel clerk was pretty good with his English.

"*Esmee Lino Rulli. Wa la thigh-ya hajj li multala lee-thay-knee.*" I'd practiced introducing myself and saying that I had a reservation for two days.

The guy behind the desk didn't seem impressed. "Sorry, do you speak English?"

"*Naam,*" I said. Yes.

"No," he said. "I think there's a problem." The clerk was a native Californian, and though I'm not sure I believe him, he told me it sounded like I'd learned *classical* Arabic, not modern Arabic. "That's why I'm having a tough time understanding you," he said. "It would be like studying Old English, not modern English."

I was speechless. In all languages.

"Do you understand me?" he said in one of those too-loud levels usually reserved for foreigners.

It took a moment for his words to sink in. I was speaking like William Shakespeare in the twenty-first century.

"Does this mean," I asked, "that I've spent the last several weeks learning phrases like 'I have a reservation' that really mean 'My Lord, dost thou havest my confirmation for lodging?' Spoken, undoubtedly, with a horrible accent, which made things even more difficult to understand?"

"*Naam,*" he said with a smile.

At least I knew *that* word.

Five years later, I visited the country of Jordan. By then I had accepted the fact that the phrase—"I beg of thee that thou dost not remove my head from my body"—wouldn't come in handy. I wouldn't be speaking their language, and they might not be speaking mine.

I was walking the streets of Amman one night, looking for a place to eat dinner. Ramadan had just ended, which meant the majority of the population had spent almost a month without water, food, or sex from sunrise to sunset. These people know how to fast!

Considering that I'm not very adventurous when it comes to fasting—which, for a Catholic, is defined as one full meal and two smaller meals not large enough to add up to a full meal—I didn't know how adventurous I'd be in my eating. But then I stumbled upon a pizza place in Amman. And, as we all know, Ammanian pizza is *the* best pizza, right? There was no one in the restaurant but three Jordanians. This was my type of place.

After pointing at the pizza I wanted, I asked the waiter to point me in the direction of the restroom: "Bathroom?" I said in perfect English. It was in the back of the restaurant. After easing my nature, as the Bible describes it, I passed by the only other table and nearly jumped when I saw what appeared to be a skull on a plate. At which point I almost eased my nature again, this time into my pants.

It was a skull, teeth and all, on a silver platter. I imagined for a moment that Salome had just finished dancing and this was the result.

Oh God, I thought. *I hope that's not a human skull or I really should have practiced how to say, "I beg of thee that thou dost not remove my head from my body."*

As I walked nervously by, one of the guys smiled and pointed at the skull.

"What is?" I asked. I have a tendency to use minimal English in the Middle East so that I can pretend I'm a foreigner just trying out English myself.

The three men smiled and, in Arabic, spoke to me—while pointing to an empty chair. I translated that into them inviting me to sit down. Of course, for all I know, they said, "Whatever you do, don't sit in this chair!" But I sat down, nonetheless.

They cut off a piece of flesh from the skull's cheekbone and put it on a plate for me. "What is?" I asked again. They answered in Arabic. The look on my face must have communicated, in a language they understood, that I still didn't understand their language.

One of the guys figured out how to explain it to me. "Baaah, baaah," he said.

"A sheep?" I asked him. I don't know why I said "sheep" since, if he knew the word, he would have said it.

Lucky for me, sheep the world over speak the same language. And whether I wanted to or not, I was going to eat one of their heads. I spent the rest of the night laughing, not talking, with these strangers in a strange land. Appreciating that they had no more intention to chop my head off than I did theirs.

When I woke up the next morning, I discovered that sheep's head didn't agree with my stomach, and I found myself quickly learning *hamaam,* the Arabic word for bathroom. Still, I wouldn't trade the night at the Ammanian pizza place for anything. Sometimes words aren't necessary to enjoy spending time with others. Or even with God. Our Father. Who is in Heaven.

CHAPTER TWENTY-FIVE

WILL YOU SAY YES?

IN APRIL OF 2008, POPE
Benedict the Seventeenth (sorry, force of habit; I mean the Sixteenth)
traveled to the United States for events in Washington, DC, and New
York City. A papal youth rally in Yonkers, New York, was scheduled near
the end of his tour, which coincided with the third anniversary of his
election to the papacy, and I'd been asked to emcee the event. Twenty-five
thousand people would gather to watch me master the ceremonies. And I
learned I'd be paid the going rate for big papal events: nothing.

On the morning of the rally, a limousine picked me up at my Manhattan
apartment at 8:00 A.M. sharp. Arriving at St Joseph's Seminary in the
Dunwoodie section of Yonkers, I was ushered through a series of security
checkpoints. The sign on my car read, "Pope's MC." I was feeling like a
rap star. I wished I had gold teeth. Lazy Lin would have been proud.

Though I didn't have a posse, I did have a handler. He pointed to a
tricked-out bus. "That's Kelly Clarkson's," he said. She was booked to sing
"Ave Maria" for the Holy Father. My main responsibility was to introduce
her. And, though not finalized, I would also introduce the pope. Not that
he needs much of an introduction, which would make my job even easier.

"That's your bus," my handler said, pointing to a slightly less tricked-
out vehicle. "It's fully stocked with food, beverages, whatever you need.
Enjoy yourself! When it's time for you to go onstage, we'll come get you."

Now I knew I had made it. I had my own tour bus, perhaps stocked full of gin and juice if they took this MC thing as far as I hoped they would. When I walked in, four assistants were waiting to serve me.

"I'm Lino," I said, resisting the urge to fist bump my staff. It was important to keep perspective, to be polite to the little people. It would probably help them if I explained the significance of my role. "I'm the emcee."

One by one, all four of them introduced themselves. It turned out that my "assistants" were actually local and national television folks. All of them were emcees, too. Awkward. Still, when it came to emcee hierarchy, I'd be introducing Kelly Clarkson, who would be singing an anthem to the Queen of the Universe, which, no doubt trumped whatever small role they would play. And did I mention, there was a chance I'd be introducing the pope?

A while later, my handler arrived with a script. It was straightforward, containing one poorly thought-out joke. Perhaps he sensed my rapper vibe because he warned me: "Stick to the wording, don't ad lib, and don't be too energetic." It was good preparation for a future role as a presenter at the Oscars.

I went over my lines a few times. Pretty simple stuff. Say some things about the pope; introduce Kelly; exit stage right.

An hour went by. Then two hours. Three hours. My assistant emcees were coming and going, introducing a variety of Christian music acts to keep the crowds energized before the Holy Father arrived.

Finally, my handler returned. "Lino, they're ready for you." My knees were shaking in the face of reality: Twenty-five thousand people were ready for me.

Backstage, I was introduced to Kelly. She was as sweet and normal as she seemed on *American Idol* back when I voted for her so many times that I was cut off by the system. She and I talked as her team of handlers did her makeup and styled her hair. From backstage, we gazed out at the mass of humanity that was the crowd. Seminarians were body surfing. A beach ball emblazoned with *Viva il Papa* bounced from one section to the next. Kelly laughed. Neither of us had ever seen anything similar to this kind of excitement, especially not for a German octogenarian.

Like an evil beach ball, my handler bounced out of nowhere with some unfortunate news. "Rulli," he said, "You're no longer introducing Kelly." She was sweet enough to say, "*Aww*" for my sake. As if that wasn't enough, he told me I wouldn't be introducing the pope, either. It was my turn to say "*Aww*."

"So what am I going to do instead?"

"Well," he paused. This wasn't going to be good. "We need you to go onstage and fire up the crowd. Most importantly, stall."

They already seemed fired up, but I was willing to pour jet fuel on the flames. "When?" I asked, needing time to prepare some material.

"Now!" He said, pointing to the empty stage.

He wanted me to stand in front of twenty-five thousand people and fill the emptiness.

That's when it struck me. I had an epiphany bigger than the tour bus I had to share with strangers. *I* couldn't fill the emptiness. Because it wasn't about *me*. In many ways, it wasn't about the headliner either. The crowds weren't there for Joseph Ratzinger; they were there for the Vicar of Christ, the successor of St. Peter. They were there for God.

And so, in a very un-Lino-like move—which could be defined as a very *saintly* move—I made it not about me. I made it about my Christian brothers and sisters who'd gathered to celebrate God's grace.

I walked onto the stage and was shocked by the size of the crowd. People as far as my eyes could see.

I began by thanking the musician, Matt Maher, who'd just been on stage. "Let's hear it for Matt Maher!" I yelled. Tens of thousands of people cheered and clapped. I was hoping it would help me stall for some time to brainstorm.

"My name is Lino Rulli," I continued. "I'm the host of a show called *The Catholic Guy.*" Whoops, that was about me. Even those of us on the way to sainthood suffer relapses. As my reward, a few hundred people pity-clapped. A lone "Yay!" could be heard.

"Three years ago today the Holy Father was elected. '*Habemus Papam!*'" I shouted. The crowd roared. This was good. "Let me hear you say it, because very soon we'll have the pope here. Say it for me now! *Habemus Papam!*"

"*Habemus Papam!*" they yelled.

Not making it about me was pretty cool. I thought I'd try for a joke. "If I knew how to speak Latin, I'd put that in the future tense, because very soon we'll have the pope here. I'm sorry I don't know how to say 'we will have a pope' in Latin. I'll work on that for the next youth rally." Another small relapse, but not as big as the one before. This was progress.

In my battle to not make it about me, I scanned the faces of the folks in the crowd. "Where are the priests?" I asked. "The men who said *yes* to the calling. Let's hear it for our priests out there. The priests who said *yes.*" A decent amount of applause.

I turned to the ladies. "Let's hear it for the sisters. The sisters all over the place—let's hear it for the sisters who said *yes.*" Even more applause.

"And let's hear it for our seminarians"—the crowd roared so loud that I doubt they heard what I said next—"who will be saying *yes.* Who are open to saying *yes.*"

Focusing on my fellow members of the body of Christ, instead of on myself, was actually strengthening me.

"The Church is not a Church of 'no, don't do this, don't do that.' The Church is a Church of 'yes.' The Holy Father said yes three years ago today. He actually said, 'Yeah, I'd like to retire, I'd like to go back to Germany, but the Lord is calling, so I'm saying yes.' The 265th successor to St. Peter is going to be right there!" I pointed to the chair he'd be sitting in, and the crowd roared again.

Next, I reminded them of one of the first things the pope said after he was elected. "The Church is young and the Church is alive." Internally, I'd transformed from rapper to revivalist. I was yelling. The crowd was yelling back.

"Now a lot of people at a youth rally say, you know, this is really great, this is the future of the Church. That's true, you are the future of the Church, but more importantly: You *are* the Church. You *will* be the future of the Church, and you *are* the Church right now. Just like the priests, just like the seminarians, just like the sisters, just like our Holy Father, God is calling each one of us to say yes to something. And one of the beautiful things about having the pope here, is that when he's speaking to each one of us, God is talking to us through Peter."

I was getting serious, and the crowd was seriously staying with me. "The Lord is going to be asking each of us to do something a little differently. But whatever it is…will you say yes when God calls you? Let me hear you, will you say yes?"

"Yes!" they screamed in return.

I saw an opening for a joke. "Good. I'm happy to hear that. Would have been really weird, actually, if everyone said, 'Eh, not so much, not so excited.'" A few laughed, but it was clear that irony and sarcasm don't work at youth rallies.

I got the sign to wrap it up. My service of stalling was over. As I walked off the stage, I resisted the urge to spread my arms out, drop my microphone to the ground, and yell, "Sexual Chocolate!" No doubt, many in my audience wouldn't have gotten or remembered the reference to Eddie Murphy's *Coming to America.* It was another heroic act on my way to canonization.

As I exited, my handler whispered in my ear, "We have to clear the backstage area because the pope is arriving. But there's room for one person right next to the bishops. Stand right there and you'll get to meet the pope when he goes by."

Looking around at my brothers and sisters standing backstage, I realized that every one of them would love to meet the pope. And so, I offered my space to someone else.

"You sure?" my handler asked.

Of course I wasn't. "Yeah," I said. "Let someone else meet Benedict. They'll remember it the rest of their lives."

Although it wasn't exactly giving my life for another person, it felt like a tiny act of heroic charity. The saintly thing to do. The Christian life isn't always built on the big, monumental decisions. Holiness can come through small acts, the habitual decision to do good things for others without expecting to receive recognition or thanks in return.

So on that day, I did good. I made the event about others, not about me. And for that, I hope to be rewarded. Of course, I probably just negated any good I did by recording the story of it in this chapter. I'm a work in progress.

CHAPTER TWENTY-SIX

KISS MY NOSE

I WAS A REALLY GREAT-LOOKING baby. I had big brown eyes and a wonderful, innocent smile. When I started first grade, I was regularly referred to as "adorable." Through my grade school years, I was eventually downgraded to decent-looking. My eyes weren't nearly as big and brown; my hair began to develop cowlicks (a funny word, but it messed up my overall feathered look).

In the sixth grade I looked like a cross between Ralph Macchio and Scott Baio. In fact, if *The Karate Kid* and *Charles in Charge* had had a kid, it would have looked like me. But then puberty struck. Damn you, puberty! And damn you, science, for not allowing Ralph Macchio and Scott Baio to have a child!

At the end of sixth grade, I went home for the summer with a normal nose. When I showed up for the first day of seventh grade, in addition to the normal changes that accompany becoming a man, I suddenly had a huge nose. Unlike the other changes that my body was experiencing, the school nurse didn't take me aside to explain the troubling changes I was noticing in the middle region of my face. And why didn't I see a growth spurt in my eyes, ears, or teeth? Not that I wanted bigger teeth or giant ears. But suddenly I was all nose, all the time.

For a long time, I hated my nose. But it was through my nose that I've come to realize that God's Word is true.

"But wait, Lino," you may want to argue. "Isn't God's Word true without your nose? You can't possibly mean that! What are you really trying to say?"

Well, of course, the Holy Scriptures are true. Period. (By the way, it's weird writing *period* instead of just "." But I wanted to get my point across.) The Bible doesn't need me to back up its validity, but it's the saint's job to make the Scriptures come alive. And being a saint, I will do so. In 2 Corinthians 12:9, there's a seemingly contradictory line: "I will all the more gladly boast of my weaknesses, that the power of Christ may rest upon me."

Boast of my weakness? Gladly.

It was a Saturday morning in the summer of 1985. My dad, in his quest to have the most attractive-looking home in our neighborhood, insisted that I do a series of outdoor chores every weekend. First on his list was the lawn. It began with a half-mile walk to the gas station in order to get a few gallons of petrol. I'd walk back, lugging the heavy container that didn't have a top on it. As if I were dropping breadcrumbs, I spilled gas all along the way. If I'd gotten lost on the way back, my parents could have simply lit a match to find me.

Once home, it was time to mow the lawn. This was the easiest and most enjoyable of the tasks, so I took my time, hoping for the rapture or some other pleasant event which would allow me to avoid the rest of the day's tasks.

Next up, the lawn needed to be edged. I'd go to the garage and look around for the edger. Even though it had only been a week since I'd used it, my dad had a tendency to reorganize the garage every few days—maybe just to confuse me. And he insisted that every tool in the garage be treated with the utmost respect due to its age. More importantly, he refused to buy new ones. The edger was no exception. It was simply a long piece of wood with a blade on the end that was meant to make a clean *edge* between the lawn and the walkway. Who, other than my dad, cared about this concept of edging the lawn, I had no idea. The wood of the ancient edger was slowly rotting away, as old as the wood of the cross itself. The metal edge hadn't been sharpened since back in the days when blacksmiths were doing brisk business. In fact, every tool in our garage seemed to have been destined for the Museum of Thankless Hard Work. Nonetheless, I always edged carefully along the sidewalk, making for a perfectly trimmed lawn.

The final task was to sweep the street. We lived on a corner, with a bus stop right in front of our house. Naturally, sand, dirt, and broken glass accumulated over time, but Pops found that to be unacceptable. And even though it was a busy city street, every Saturday I became a human Frogger, cleaning the street while dodging in and out of traffic.

All of this grueling work was made easier thanks to my portable Walkman and Eddie Murphy's comedy album (well, cassette in my case) *Delirious*. That summer, I learned every one of his jokes by heart. I loved when he talked about his family. "Does anyone have a mother that would hit you with a shoe? By the time I was ten, my mother was like Clint Eastwood with a shoe" always killed me. And made me glad neither of my parents threw shoes at me.

Just as I was finishing my street cleaning that day, a black Cadillac Seville pulled up along the freshly swept street. Two guys in their early twenties with sweet mustaches and feathered hairdos yelled for me to come over. I figured these two classy dudes were looking for directions to the local high school where they would pick up chicks—or to the local Kwik-E-Mart where they would hang out and buy alcohol for minors.

I tried to play it cool as I turned off my Walkman and approached the car. "Yeah, man. What's up?"

The driver revved the engine. "BIG NOSE!" they yelled, tearing off before I could respond.

Ahh, yes. There's nothing like a heartfelt, out-of-the-blue insult after a long day of yard work. I only wished my mom had been there to throw a shoe at them.

Exhausted and frustrated, I walked into our non–air-conditioned house. That was refreshing. Inside, my mom, dad, and Grandpa Rulli were sitting in the living room.

"I don't want my nose anymore," I announced. I figured between the three of them, at least one could be blamed for my schnoz.

My dad was the first to answer. "Lino," he said, "you're Italian."

It wasn't a groundbreaking explanation. My mom and grandpa nodded in agreement. The implication seemed to be: *I was Italian, after all, so this is what I deserved.*

Running upstairs, I went into my bedroom and closed the door behind me. I looked in the mirror above my dresser. I looked at my nose. My skin. My forehead. And then my eyes. They weren't as big and brown as when I was a kid. But I stared into my own eyes for several minutes. I wasn't looking at myself in the mirror superficially; I was looking inside myself.

I saw Lino Rulli, the dork with a giant nose, sweaty and uncomfortable in his own skin. The very opposite of the guys in the Seville. I wish *my name was John Smith. I wish I had an average-sized nose. I wish my hair would feather. I wish I was 6'7" tall and 240 pounds of pure muscle. Life would be so much easier. Dudes would pull up to my house and just yell,* "BIG!"

*   *   *

Life with my nose hasn't gotten easier. But now I've come to understand how in my weakness I find my strength. I can boast about the size of my nose. What once was mocked now is praised.

It no longer bothers me that when I walk into a room, the first thing people's eyes focus on is my nose. I don't even mind the fact that my nose enters a room before the rest of my body does. And I'm OK with the fact that I can't go for a swim in the ocean, doing the backstroke, without someone yelling, "Shark!"

All right, those might be slight exaggerations. But this isn't: There are very few drinking glasses that I can fit my nose into. When I buy glassware, I have to ask the sales clerk to help me find my size. Thankfully, when in Ireland and treating myself to a Guinness, the wide-mouthed pint is no problem for my nose; there's enough room for my beak in that.

But if I'm at a gathering where we toast with champagne—and that champagne is in a flute—I have to lean my head back and just pour the booze in. My nose isn't even close to fitting in. It's like a blockade that won't allow the liquor to touch my lips.

And here's another charming aspect of my nose: It runs a lot. I blow my nose about ten times a day, not because there's a lot there. But because there's always just a little, teeny bit.

Ever since the seventh grade, I've kept the Kleenex close at hand. (I refuse to carry a handkerchief, because how gross is that? Why would I want an embroidered snot rag?) In high school I was on the wrestling team, but knowing I'd have to occasionally blow my nose, I'd always keep a Kleenex in my sock. Before hitting the mat, I'd blow my nose quickly, and then begin to wrestle.

To this day, I have a Kleenex in my back pocket at all times.

And what's even better? I get bloody noses about twice a year. It usually happens at inopportune times. In 2003, I got back together with a girl I'd broken up with two years before. We had dated, broken up, and she went out with someone else, but the minute they broke up, there I was. It wasn't like I was stalking her. I was just casually in the bushes every night because I enjoy sleeping in jagged thornbushes. Don't judge.

On our first reunited date, I drove over to her place to pick her up for dinner. It was a beautiful home; clearly she was doing better financially than when we last dated. I knocked at the door, thinking, *This is it, Lino. Don't screw it up.* The way my mind races, I can move ahead pretty quickly. Like, we'll fall back in love, and maybe someday I'll carry her through the door of this beautiful house as her husband. (Notice I moved into her place? Told you it was really nice.)

We went out to an Italian restaurant. I ordered a simple pasta dish with cheese in browned butter. "I'll have the same," she said, to my delight.

"And for drinks?" The waiter asked.

I ordered my favorite drink at the time: Captain Morgan and Coke. She ordered the same. What a classy girl! I remembered why we liked each other: We had so much in common.

After dinner, I drove her back to her house and walked her back to that beautiful front door. We had been talking about Jerry Seinfeld earlier that night, and she had been bragging about her videotape collection. (This was before boxed sets of DVDs were available, and before the show was in heavy syndication, so if you wanted to watch *Seinfeld,* you had to video-tape them when you had the chance.)

"Do you want to come inside?" she asked. Her hand reached out to touch my arm.

"Yeah, I'd love to," I said. And then, at that very moment, a drop of blood fell from my nose and onto her wrist. Then some drops fell on her forearm. It wasn't as sexy as it sounds.

After running into what could have been *my* house for what could have been a roll of *my* paper towels, I offered to leave.

She agreed.

I was left staring at a closed door.

* * *

God gave me a giant nose for a reason, but it took me a long time to understand that. And now? I see it as a blessing, not a curse. But I had to give it time. That's how life is; we have to wait and let God's plan unfold. I finally see how God could use my nose. Instead of loathing it, I began loving it.

When I had the opportunity to start a television production company, instead of calling it *Lino's Productions*, I decided on *Linose Productions*. The name takes away people's power to hurt me. In my weakness I can be strong. And my nose is in everything I do, anyway.

Perhaps the craziest thing about me embracing my nose is that others now embrace my nose. Metaphorically and literally. I've had women kiss my nose. They've told me it's sexy or distinctive. I've had guys take pictures with my nose. Some folks are even jealous of my nose. Jealous of *my nose!* I guess it allows me to be unique; I stand out in a crowd. In other words, the things I thought were my flaws have become my strengths. What defined me in the negative now defines me in the positive. Weakness can be celebrated. In my life, and in the life of the Church.

I belong to a Church that I thoroughly love, despite the fact that it is very, very weak. Power-hungry cardinals, crazy nuns, hypocritical laypeople. Weak people, all of them. All of them struggling to overcome their weaknesses. And I'm happy to stand right alongside them with my weaknesses.

I can't overcome sin. But God can. God allows these thorns in my side, and this nose on my face, so that I will keep struggling and sharing my struggles. We all have weaknesses, and that's where God comes in.

The saints thank God for who they are, for how wonderfully God created them, and for how their flaws as well as their strengths glorify Him. Instead of wishing He had made me differently, I thank Him for making me just the way He did.

My nose magnifies the Lord. My nose rejoices in God, my Savior.

CHAPTER TWENTY-SEVEN

THE REDDEST RED
THAT RED HAD EVER BEEN

WHEN I WAS A COLLEGE student at St. John's, we celebrated the end of winter by gathering in the woods on campus to drink, do drugs, listen to bands, and dance with girls who didn't shave their armpits. We would have called this celebration "Woodstock" if the name hadn't already been taken. Instead, someone noticed a bunch of pine trees in the woods, and named the festival Pinestock. It was a university-sanctioned celebration, even though there wasn't much about it that reflected the admirable Benedictine qualities of the common good, community living, hospitality, and moderation.

My friends and I lived communally, we were hospitable, and we sometimes cared about the common good, but we weren't exactly moderate. When it came to Pinestock, our immoderation began on the Saturday morning of the festival. Our senior year, my roommates awoke early and headed to the Penalty Box, a house that got its name because a bunch of the university's hockey players lived there. (For the record, I lived in the much-less-sexy Grandma's House, so named because the one-story brick home with the plastic deer on the lawn and the lace curtains in the window looked like a place where someone's grandmother would live.)

That morning, in the living room of the Penalty Box, twenty or so guys circled a keg of beer, intent on drinking up all its goodness. This is how it always went: To save a few bucks, we bought expired beer, so there usually wasn't much goodness to consume. After a couple of beers, someone in the group would bring out some pot and we'd smoke up. But that year, our last year together, a guy named Nate showed up, and because you can't spell "ante" without "Nate," he upped it.

"It's our last Pinestock," he said, holding a Ziploc sandwich bag full of mushrooms, "so, let's do some 'shrooms." I'm not sure what hallucinogenic fungi had to do with our status as seniors but, at the time, logic wasn't important. He had mushrooms. They were in a little bag. In the interest of the common good, he was offering to share.

I knew my way around alcohol and weed. I'd tried acid but didn't like it much. It was time to make a decision: Would I try 'shrooms? I hesitated. I didn't even like them on my pizza.

"Come on, Lino," a buddy of mine said, "it's our senior year."

Considering the fact that he wasn't graduating on time and would be staying on for a fifth year, his was, by far, the least persuasive version of Nate's original argument; it was an argument with a serious flaw. In other words, peer pressure.

When it comes to peer pressure, back then and now, I seem to be pressured into doing only bad things. Rare is the time that peer pressure has me praying more, doing more charitable works, or getting me closer to heaven. If someone tries to pressure me into Eucharistic Adoration, I stand my ground. I will not be pressured to kneel in front of the presence of Jesus Christ, Body, Blood, Soul, and Divinity. Not for one holy second, definitely not for a whole hour. But if, as in the case of Pinestock, someone wants me to spend an afternoon swallowing magic mushrooms to see how messed up I could get, how could I say no? After all, it was senior year.

"Let's do it!" I said.

"Great," he said, opening up the bag to share them with all of us in the circle. But then, he paused, confused. "How much are we each supposed to take?"

We were off to a bad start. The guy who'd upped the ante didn't know by how much.

"I think an ounce," one guy said.

Another chimed in. "An ounce! Are you high?" Umm, yes, we were all high. "You'll die if you take that much."

Hold up, I thought. *Did he just say that we could die from this stuff?* Was he using *hyperbole*? And did I just use the term *hyperbole* correctly in a sentence?

"Hey, guys," I said. "If I really want to trip this bad, maybe I should just blindfold myself and walk down an uneven sidewalk." I was trying to reverse my impulsive "Let's do it!" from moments before. Unfortunately, the weakest joke in history wasn't going to save me from my stupidity.

The group concurred that a little less than half an ounce each was within the bounds of Benedictine moderation. But this decision led to more confusion for Nate.

"How do I know how much is an ounce?"

Someone tried to help him do the math. "How many ounces of 'shrooms are in the bag?"

Nate shrugged. He couldn't remember the total. And this was our leader.

Another guy proposed that we just split up the bag evenly between the twenty or so of us there. "And then, let's just see what happens!"

It seemed like a prudent plan.

Nate walked around the circle, passing out 'shrooms, doing the best he could to make it fair. Some guys got a little more, some a little less.

What would it taste like? I bit into what Nate handed me. The guy next to me did likewise.

"It tastes like a turd," he said.

He was being generous. Still, I told myself, it'd be worth it, because it was our senior year.

Before that day, I had been afraid that doing 'shrooms would make me see things that weren't there. A frog chasing me, carrying in his stubby frog hands a videotape of *Webster*, insisting that he and I spend an afternoon together on the couch watching all six seasons of the hit TV show.

Instead, for me, 'shrooms changed how I perceived the things that were there. Nate's head upped *its* ante, growing three sizes before my eyes. One friend's tongue seemed to drop from his mouth to the living room floor. Another buddy's nose mocked mine, getting smaller as I stared at it. Instead of being afraid or resentful of these transformations, I found them all absolutely, incredibly, unbelievably, hyperbolically hilarious.

It occurs to me that if you're not enjoying this book, maybe you should do some 'shrooms to help intensify the humor. (Seriously, *don't* do drugs, kids. Cue NBC "The More You Know" music here.)

I don't know what the others were seeing, but it was clear that their experiences were equally intense. My friend Mark came up with an even more intense idea. "Who wants to sit in the car?"

He was speaking of a large orange sedan that was parked out in the driveway.

As if he were Braveheart (before Mel Gibson became anti-Semitic Mel Gibson) challenging us to storm a battlefield in defense of our freedom, we roared our response, "Yeah!" And then, "Yeah." And then, "Hell, yeah." We raced to the front door and piled into the car as if it were Elijah's chariot, ready to take us on a trip to heaven. We hopped in the unlocked vehicle and realized no one had the keys. In retrospect, this was for the best. There we were, a group of guys sitting in a car, going nowhere—the metaphor completely lost on us.

Someone in the back seat said, "Hat!" and we laughed and laughed at the sheer hilarity of that word. After maybe an hour of such screaming and howling, or maybe it was only a minute—that's the problem with 'shrooms, they make you completely lose track of time—someone else had the idea of switching from driving the orange chariot to driving golf balls. Again, the suggestion was rewarded with willingness and cackling.

One of the guys, Matt, was a pretty decent golfer. He managed to find his clubs and set a ball on the tee.

Apparently his experience with 'shrooms included hallucinations of grandeur. "Who thinks I can hit the freeway?" I-94 was at least a mile away. Between it and us lay a hundred acres of rough and at least one of the ten thousand or so water hazards in the state of Minnesota—what the locals like to call "lakes." We took bets, nonetheless.

Smack! Matt hit the ball as hard as he could, watching as it sailed, and then landed about 5,130 feet short of the freeway.

"Perhaps that's why PGA players don't do 'shrooms before hitting the links," I said to more applause and shrieks. I was loving this drug. I'd never been this funny in my life. Yet, all too soon, my comedic success wore me out.

"Guys," I said. My friends laughed. "I'm going home." They roared with laughter.

"Lino, that's genius!" they cheered in unison. "Best line of the day!"

I could still hear their laughter, as I acted on the greatest one-liner of my life, turning the corner and heading for Grandma's House. On the way, I found that the road had been repainted by Salvador Dalí. Though it was a straight path only a few hours earlier, it now zigged and zagged. I stepped over a pool of goo, once a mailbox, now melted on the sidewalk. A house in the distance floated above its manicured lawn, held to the ground by only a few fraying ropes.

A few blocks into my crazytown walk, I'd made it to an oasis I recognized: the local gas station. They were having some sort of church fundraiser, with a few families milling around outside. There was a guy roasting hot dogs and a woman selling pastries. A strand of red balloons threatened to lift the whole building up to the clouds.

The woman in charge of hawking the pastries was better looking than she should have been. The guy selling hot dogs was shorter than he should have been. He was wearing a tuxedo. Naturally, I turned my attention to the hot dogs he was grilling. I could not take my eyes off them. On the outside, the links looked so succulent, so juicy, so moist. I could see inside of them, too. I won't tell you what I saw there; you don't want to know what's inside hot dogs. I'll just tell you that watching this tiny man turn his flock of hot dogs over so they cooked evenly brought me great joy. And then, as suddenly as the joy washed over me, it left, and I found myself wondering whether the dwarf—or midget, or whatever the politically correct term for him was back then or is now—whether his cumberbund and tails were evidence that I was losing my mind. Why is a dwarf in a tuxedo making hot dogs on the day I'm taking mushrooms?

By the way, I've always been jealous of dwarves. I'm jealous because they get to decide what they're called. No one asks a guy with a big nose what he'd like to be called. He's just the guy with the big beak, the huge horn, the super-sniffer. I'm jealous of unusually tall people, too. We don't wonder if they're still single because of some kind of character defect. Instead, we assume that they just haven't found a love of equal height yet, someone with whom to become equally and levelly yoked. I'm jealous of pretty much everyone else, too. Perhaps it's because I have a talent for seeing the negative in the good and the good in the negative.

In the final moments of my hot-dog-and-dwarf-staring contest, it was I who blinked first. I wanted badly to go home and take a nap.

"I'm going home to take a nap," I said to the hot dogs and then to the dwarf, neither of whom laughed as my friends had.

Later, I would learn that when a person tries mushrooms for the first time, the rule is "never be by yourself." One should always trip with people who can help guide the tripper through the impending mania. Back home at Grandma's House, I was completely alone. Anyone who should have been with me was likely back in the orange sedan, driving to nowhere.

Is that my back hair I feel growing? I asked myself. I went into the bathroom, took my shirt off, and twisted around to examine my back in the mirror. I was really freaking out. I ran to my bedroom, dove under the covers, and closed my eyes to the horror of back hair. With my eyes closed, I saw an array of colors, patterns, and what might have been trapezoids. It was then that I wished I'd studied harder in math, so that I could identify the shape that was weighing down on me.

I started to panic for real. I opened my eyes. The clock on the bedside table read 3:53 P.M. I stared at it for what felt like an hour. It never changed. There, in my bedroom in Collegeville, Minnesota, time had chosen to make its stand. And 'shrooms ceased to be fun.

"Oh God, help me."

I said it quietly at first. Perhaps I wasn't even talking to God. Perhaps I was speaking to one of the trapezoids that I could see in my mind's eye.

"God, come and help me." This time I meant it, and though I didn't see Him when I closed my eyes, I was talking to Him. And at 3:53 P.M., on the afternoon of Pinestock weekend, I saw the Sacred Heart of Jesus.

My grandfather, Gino, had a devotion to the Sacred Heart. He died the year I was born, and when I was a teenager my mom gave me the Sacred Heart prayer card he used to carry in his wallet. Even though I didn't know what it was all about, I kept it in my wallet, too. These days, I know that Jesus appeared to a seventeenth-century French nun, Margaret Mary

Alacoque, and revealed His Sacred Heart to her so that the world would know of His mercy. That afternoon, all I knew was I needed some mercy ASAP.

When I found my wallet, I pulled out my grandfather's card and focused on the Sacred Heart. Looking down on it, it seemed as if the heart was actually pounding through the card. Blood pumped through the ventricles harder than blood had ever pumped through ventricles. The red of the heart was the reddest red that red had ever been. Had I not been hallucinating, it might have been a miracle—or, at the very least, a vision.

Whatever it was, the card helped me focus my eyes on God, and this focus put me on a path to peace. My own heart started beating a little more normally. I laughed, this time prompted by the genuinely funny synchronization of sacred and human. The laughter helped. When I'm laughing, there's no room for fear. And less room for doubt.

Not knowing how many more hours I'd be tripping, I realized it would be better if I returned to my friends. The Sacred Heart of Jesus was great and all, but I needed the counsel of my community.

Walking back along the winding road, I passed the only Catholic church in town. I didn't go inside, but as I walked by, I said, "God, if you get me through this, I swear I'll never do mushrooms again." Yes, it was a narrow promise, but it was an honest prayer. And it's a promise to the Lord that I've actually kept. That, in and of itself, is a miracle. And while I didn't have a vision that day, I certainly had a revelation: In a moment of freaking out, I turned to God. I was happy about that.

Do I run to God when I'm in trouble? Absolutely. Some of my more devout Catholic friends mock atheist-in-a-foxhole moments of turning to God in an hour of need. Some of my atheist friends call religion a crutch. To both charges I say, exactly! Regardless of my sins, when I'm in a foxhole, I turn to God. When my legs are broken, I need a crutch.

I know that God won't mock me or turn His back on me, regardless of what drugs I've tried or how stupid I am. The challenge is to turn to God when I'm not in the middle of a bad trip. When I don't feel that I need Him. That's the challenge for those of us seeking sainthood. But when we sin, we have two options: despair or repentance. The saint chooses repentance.

It's tough to be in touch with what holiness really is and what sainthood really looks like, but a saint who's spent most of his life succumbing to peer pressure? A saint who's done mushrooms? And what's more, a saint that still takes some pleasure in telling the messy story? That's probably too much for a lot of pious folks to handle. None of it is saintly behavior.

Yet we've got saints who were repentant murderers, repentant prostitutes, and sometimes both. Unholy things happen in the messiness of life.

Proverbs 24:16 says, "A righteous man falls seven times, and rises again." Even though it might not be a saintly thing to do, I'd like to add to that: "When you're tripping, you'll likely fall even more. But God is always with you."

CHAPTER TWENTY-EIGHT

THERE

YEARBOOK DAY WAS A SPECIAL time at my high school. For the freshmen, sophomores, and juniors, the yearbook simply represented a chance to see who'd been caught "Dancing the Night Away" at the homecoming dance, or who'd been named "Most Likely to Have Kissed No More Than Two Girls by Graduation."

But for us graduating seniors, yearbook time was a chance to see what your parents really thought of you. It was a not-terribly-well-thought-out concept that allowed our parents to have the final word before we graduates became adults:

Dear Karen,
Your room is a mess. You have horrible taste in music. Oh, and you're
adopted.
Love,
Mom and Dad

* * *

To Don,
Your friends always thought you were a loser, and they only hung out
with you because they needed someone to drive them to and from
school. I told you to quit being a pushover. You didn't listen to me.
You should have.
Sincerely,
Dad

* * *

Tanya,

You wouldn't have ended up being the class tramp if that bum who calls himself your father had spent more time with you when you were young and you weren't looking for attention and a daddy-figure. Blame him for how you turned out.

Love,

Mom

* * *

With equal combination of fear and excitement, I found my parents' message to me:

To Lino,

"There" is not better than "here." When your "there" has become a "here," you will simply obtain another "there" that will, again, look better than "here." We're glad you were here. We wish you success when you are there.

Love,

Mom and Pops

I didn't understand their message then, but the words have always stuck with me. They saw the path I was heading on—one of longing, searching, of always being an "other"— before I started down it.

My whole life I've been trying to find my *there*. Sometimes running toward it. Sometimes running away. I have no idea what I'm running to, or who I'm running from. More accurately, away from *whom* I am running. I wish I knew. It seems the answer is as murky as a grammar rule. But I think I have a clue.

In my previous book, *Sinner* (available at Amazon.com or wherever fine books…wait, if you still don't have a copy, you're never gonna buy one), I recounted the story of how my dad left his job at a correctional facility to become an organ grinder. He was the hurdy-gurdy man, grinding his organ for all to see. I was his assistant, a.k.a., the Monkey Boy, and I spent much of my adolescence following Pops through local fairgrounds and parades.

But, of course, there's more to the story.

When I was fifteen, I'd just gotten home from school one day when my dad ambushed me at my weakest moment: while I was looking for the television remote.

"Lino, you know you're my favorite son." He usually opened with this line when he needed something. The tip-off was the fact that I am an only child. So when he called me his favorite, I got nervous.

"What do you need?" I asked, presuming the worst.

"I don't need anything from you," he said. "But I want to give you something. You won't believe it, but I've been offered a once-in-a-lifetime organ-grinding opportunity."

I pointed out that, as an organ grinder, he was already living a once-in-a-lifetime opportunity. How many lives does he need?

He continued, with a big smile on his face. "You've heard the phrase, 'I'm going to run away and join the circus,' right?"

I shook my head no. I hadn't heard of the phrase, but I was anxious to know why he was using a line no one was really saying.

"Well," he said, both proudly and nervously, "I got a phone call to join the circus."

"When?"

"They called me yesterday."

Pops and I have always struggled to communicate even the simplest of information. "No," I clarified, "I'm not asking when they called. I'm asking when they want you to join the circus."

"Now," he said. "And not just me. You, too."

"Join the circus tomorrow?" I asked. "I can't! I've got a math test..." As soon as the words were out of my mouth, I realized that perhaps *that's* where the phrase "run away and join the circus" had originated: getting out of taking math tests. What kid, when given the choice between measuring the circumference of a ring or performing in one, would choose the former? And so, math tests be damned, I said yes. Time to live out that not-exactly-cliché phrase: I'd run away and join the circus.

The next morning, while Pops went down to the school to make my excuses, Mom hurriedly packed for me—some clothes, toiletries, and a camera to record all these special memories. I promised to call her as soon as we arrived at the hotel. She kissed me on the cheek and said she loved me. And I figure she must have loved my dad and I very much, because what other wife and mother allows two-thirds of her family to leave like this?

Then Pops was back home, grabbing his organ and his keys and urging us to hurry up with the good-byes. As I picked up my bag, I wondered what I was forgetting. But there was no time to make sure that my bag contained everything a future circus performer would need. We were flying out the door. We were heading west to join the circus.

The Ringling Brothers and Barnum & Bailey Circus? No, we didn't join a circus you've actually heard of. That would have been too easy. Too dignified.

Three rings? Very ostentatious. Not tough enough for us Rullis.

We were headed for a small, yet classy, one-ringed spectacle: Circus Flora, an honest-to-God traveling circus complete with trapeze artists, acrobats, trained animals, and musicians. The most famous act was a group called the Flying Wallendas. They'd been doing death-defying high-wire acts for generations—all without a net—and were legendary.

This was the crew who awaited us when Pops and I made it to our first city: Keystone, Colorado, a quiet ski town with a population less than my high school. It was springtime, and it hadn't snowed in a while. The Keystoners were hungry for entertainment.

I looked at my environment and thought about the fact that only a few days ago I was stuck in school, struggling to memorize the rules of scientific notation. And now I noted that there seemed to be no rules.

"Lino, I'd like you to meet Flora," the show's director said. "You two will be working together."

Flora was a baby elephant. As in the *Circus Flora*. I would be riding the show's namesake as part of the grand finale. That's why I dropped out of school: to ride an elephant around a one-ring circus.

I'm not sure why they chose me to do this, but I was happy to see someone—or something—with a snout larger than mine.

Like any performer, I knew I'd have to bond with my colleague. I introduced myself using the same clever line that in a few years I would be trying on girls at bars. "Hey Flora, my name is Lino." She gave me a preview of the kinds of responses I could expect. She stared at me. Then she took a dump.

Yet, as we trained together, we grew closer. I found her to be a surprisingly calm beast. She and I shared the best kind of conversations—I talked and she listened. She was the perfect companion, listening patiently to my meanderings and theories about all sorts of things. I'd give her some food, she'd take another enormous dump, and then it was time for rehearsal.

"OK, Flora, here we go." This was my signal that the witty banter was over. It was time to saddle up and perform. But because she wasn't a horse, saddling up wasn't as easy as I'd imagined. In fact, there was no saddle. Instead, I had to set up a rickety stepladder in the space between her front leg and her rib cage, climb up the ladder, and hope she was still with me when I got to the top.

"You ready?" I'd ask, ready to leave the stepladder and become an elephant rider. The first time I tried it, she walked away. There I was, standing on top of a ladder, with no place to go. I'd step down, move the stepladder to wherever she went, and persevere.

"Let's try that again, OK?" I'd say. And once again, she moved away. She walked away from me a few more times, until, I suppose, she decided the joke was getting stale. Soon enough, I hopped aboard and began riding an elephant. No saddle, no reins. She could buck me off whenever she wanted. Nothing but her kindness stood between me and the ground.

After several days of practice, we were ready for opening night. From backstage, I watched the performers. They were amazing. They loved their craft. They *lived* for their craft. One of my favorites was an acrobat who was missing a thumb. Which is neither here nor there—just a fun detail.

Since the circus was named after Flora, we were the closing act. When it was our turn, I climbed aboard her, the curtains opened, and we made our grand entrance into the ring.

Everyone loved the baby elephant so much that no one seemed to care that we weren't actually performing. It was just a big-nosed teenager riding an elephant. Kids laughed and waved at her, and sometimes at me. My dad, the organ grinder, played along as she walked the perimeter of the ring for her adoring fans.

Then all the performers would come out and take a final bow, we'd head backstage, and my workday was over…as soon as someone remembered to bring the stepladder over and coax Flora into letting me down. Sometimes it took a while.

A few nights into the run of the show, an aftershow party was held in a local condominium. It was the stuff of my dreams: exotic animals, acrobatic women, and alcohol.

"Do you want a beer, Lino?" my dad asked me.

Up to this point in my life, I'd only consumed alcohol *without* my parents' permission. It was odd having my dad actually offer me some. I wondered if it would taste different.

"Thanks, Pops," I said, holding a cold Budweiser. I cracked it open and drank it slowly. I felt I had become a man.

As I chatted with my fellow performers, I heard a voice say, "I'm going outside onto the deck...and into the hot tub." That was Natasha, a Russian gymnast, whose name (and everything else about her) was so nice that I couldn't believe we were the same age. She was mature beyond her years—physically and emotionally.

"Am I going out by myself?" she asked coyly.

It was a wraparound deck, tucked away from the rest of the party, which meant whoever was out there with Natasha would be by themselves. And it was a two-person hot tub. Which meant I'd be fighting off clowns, animal trainers, and more clowns. But to be near Natasha, it was worth it. Maybe I'd become a man in another way that night. And as you know from chapter twenty, I liked hot tubs as an adult. As a teenager, I liked them even more when they had Russian gymnasts in them.

I would be with a woman who could contort her body in ways my mind could only dream. I imagined her long legs wrapping around me. She was a snake; I was her prey.

And then I saw her. "Lino, what a nice surprise," she said, as I found myself able to find some private time with her and I too-eagerly jumped into the tub, splashing water everywhere. "I was afraid I'd be out here all alone."

And then I saw *her*. That's when the miracle happened. I didn't see her as an object, or someone whose attractiveness was based on her flexibility. Thoughts of lust turned to thoughts of love. The love God has for all of us, and especially her. Here was a woman who deserved the love and acceptance that I so desperately crave. Not based on what we do, or what we have to do to make others like us, but simply based on who we are.

Natasha and I just…talked. And I was happy with that. In short, I didn't sin. Let me repeat that. I was a teenage boy, in a hot tub with a pretty acrobat teenage girl—who felt alone—and I committed no sin at all. We talked about family and friends back home; our hopes and dreams for the future. We were just two kids trying not to feel so alone in the world.

That's it. I think you'll agree I deserve canonization now. Because while it's true that I didn't really become a man that night, other than the Budweiser, I think that's the night I became a saint.

* * *

We traveled across the country, from Colorado to New York. Being on the road, traveling from city to city, I got used to the strange routine. It soon defined my sense of normality. And I liked it. These were my people. That was my elephant. We'd plant roots for a few days, do a few shows, pack up, and move on to the next city.

When I look back on my life, music and TV were obviously enormous influences. But then there was the circus. The circus trained me to ride an elephant, but it also left me feeling uncomfortable staying in a place for too long.

It's probably why I have this wanderlust for travel. It doesn't matter where I'm going, as long as I'm going somewhere. When I lived in Minnesota, I loved going to New York to visit; now that I live in New York, I love going to Minnesota. Even when it's six degrees. Below zero. Indoors. And that's in the summertime.

I can't help but wonder if my fear of commitment—especially with women—goes back to that training in the circus, as well. I perform. I entertain. I revel in the accolades, but when I sense that I'm just about to lose the love of my audience, I pack up the tent and leave.

That same fear of commitment has probably kept me from fully discerning my vocation, too. Only now do I wonder how different I'd have turned out if I'd run away and joined a seminary.

Ever since my days as a circus performer, I've been running. Moving. Looking for a *there*—as my parents put it—instead of being *here*. And yet, as I get older, I get more and more concerned that I haven't found my *there* yet.

My prayers are increasingly becoming a sort of "Keep me out of the 'In Memoriam' segment of life for a little while longer, Lord, and I'll do my best to put the pieces together. I'll do what I can to make something of the mess that is my existence. Also, if a movie is ever made of my life, can Keanu Reeves play me in the film?"

There was a time in my life when I thought I'd change the world. Now I'm starting to wonder if I can even change...me. I'm still the shy, insecure sinner who just wants to fit *in* this world.

I'd love to tell you this book wraps up because I'm now at peace. Truth is, that's the way most religious books wrap up—they tell you how to find that peace. But, let's be honest, if that were the case, this book would be a lot more pious. *I'd* be a lot more pious.

Instead, I can say that I definitely know what it's like to be a sinner. But I'd rather be a saint.

So I end this book with another confession: In spite of my best efforts, I know I'll never be canonized by the Church. I'll be lucky if, through God's grace and mercy, I'm counted among those in heaven.

And that's the one thing that ultimately brings me some comfort: I've come to realize that my *there* is actually heaven. So *here* is never going to be a place I'm completely comfortable with. (It seems my parents were right. Don't you hate when that happens?)

Sometimes you chase me, Lord. Sometimes I chase you. But the only time I'll quit running, the only time I will finally feel at peace, will be when I'm at home with you: there in heaven. That's when I'll truly be called a saint.

About the Author

Lino Rulli is a three-time Emmy winner and host of *The Catholic Guy* on SiriusXM Satellite Radio. He is also personal media advisor to Cardinal Timothy Dolan. In his free time, he enjoys staring at a blank white wall with a glass of boxed red wine in one hand, and a turkey leg in the other. He lives a rich, full life.